IN THE SPIRIT OF DEMOCRACY

Politics and Attitudes

Seen from my point of view

By
George Manus

Author: George Manus
Copyright: George Manus
Design and Layout: Ole Praud
Illustrations: George Manus

Publisher:
BoD · Books on Demand, Strandvejen 100, 2900 Hellerup,
bod@bod.dk

Tryk:
Libri Plureos GmbH, Friedensallee 273, 22763 Hamborg,
Tyskland

George's online bookstore:
www.georgemanus-books.com

The Art of George Manus online store:
www.georgemanus.com

George's innovation & hub website:
www.maxmanusinnovation.com

Email: info@georgemanus.com

ISBN: 978-87-7145-788-9

Other books written by George Manus

THOUGHTS   English
TANKER   Norwegian

REFLECTIONS I   English
REFLEKSJONER I   Norwegian

REFLECTIONS II   English
REFLEKSJONER II Norwegian

REFLECTIONS III English
REFLEKSJONER III Norwegian

A WOMAN'S MANY MIGRATIONS   English
EN KVINNES MANGE FLYTTINGER   Norwegian

STORIES & THOUGHTS I   English
HISTORIER OG TANKER I   Norwegian

STORIES & THOUGHTS II   English
HISTORIER OG TANKER II Norwegian

INNOVATIONS AND CREATIONS English

MAX MANUS FIRMAENE -70 år i kommunikasjon Norwegian

WORDS FOR THE ROAD - ORD MED PÅ VEIEN I   English - Norwegian
WORDS FOR THE ROAD - ORD MED PÅ VEIEN II   English - Norwegian
WORDS FOR THE ROAD - ORD MED PÅ VEIEN III   English - Norwegian
WORDS FOR THE ROAD - ORD MED PÅ VEIEN IV   English - Norwegian
WORDS FOR THE ROAD - ORD MED PÅ VEIEN V   English - Norwegian
WORDS FOR THE ROAD - ORD MED PÅ VEIEN VI   English - Norwegian
WORDS FOR THE ROAD - ORD MED PÅ VEIEN VII   English - Norwegian
WORDS FOR THE ROAD - ORD MED PÅ VEIEN VIII   English - Norwegian
WORDS FOR THE ROAD - ORD MED PÅ VEIEN IX   English - Norwegian
WORDS FOR THE ROAD - ORD MED PÅ VEIEN X   English - Norwegian

FOOD FOR THOUGHTS - 1001 Short reflections   English
TANKEVEKKERE - 1001 korte refleksjoner   Norwegian

217 REFLECTONS - Reflections on big and small   English
217 REFLEKSJONER - Refleksjoner over stort og smått Norwegian

"THE MISCHIEVOUS BOY Boy"and the War Heroe   English
"RAMPEGUTTEN" og Krigshelten   Norwegian

MY LIFE VALUES I   English
MY LIFE VALUES II   English

MINE LIVSVERDIER I   Norwegian
MINE LIVSVERDIER II   Norwegian

INTRODUCTION

March 2025

I have given this book the same title I had for a Reflection I wrote in 2016 and called:

IN THE SPIRIT OF DEMOCRACY.

It is taken from my book: 217 Reflections, published in 2022, is only about five pages long, and represent some of my political views at the time it was written.

When I read it today, almost ten year later, I largely stand by what I wrote then.

After **IN THE SPIRIT OF DEMOCRACY** follows a small report: **A DAY TO BE REMEMBERED,** which I wrote in June 2024, and which in my opinion speaks for itself.

Then, from my book "**FOOD FOR THOUGHT** - 1001 short reflections", which was published in 2020, I have selected 84 that are all in one way or another related to politics, and are named in the table of contents in alphabetical order.

All the Food for Thought are short and usually only a few lines long.

As I have now passed eighty-five and have been permanent resident in Spain for the last fifteen to twenty years, some of the political Food for Thought will naturally bear the imprint of that, but mainly, and from my point of view, I believe that they reflect my personal opinions.

As far back as I can remember, I have been concerned with people's attitudes and not least in the recent years I have become much more aware if this, not least in light of the fact that, as mentioned, I have lived in Spain for many years and in the last 10 published 24 books.

In my opinion, it should be a requirement for politicians

elected in democratic societies that they are equipped with solid and fair life values and attitudes at all levels, as they are elected to govern society for us taxpayers.

From my selection of Reflections, I have included 34, all of which are to a greater or lesser extent related to Life Values and Attitudes. The first was written in 1990 and the last in 2023. They were put on paper to test my opinions about Life Values and Attitudes.

After each Reflection, which covers from two to five pages, I have, except in a few with more, inserted four Food for Thought, related to the content of the respective Reflection.

I have chosen to include these Reflections and Food for Thought, many of which are strongly personal, because I see Life Values and Attitudes as man's most important management tool.

I do not claim in any way that these reflections are the solution for the most important and correct life values and attitudes, but that they may provide a small reminder of their importance for all of us and not least for those who deal with politics.

George Manus

IN THE SPIRIT OF DEMOCRACY

June 2016

The word democracy means parliamentary rule.

The people in democratically ruled countries decide the policy to be conducted. The political party having the majority, either formed by its own voters, or by coalitions, largely determines the policy to be conducted as long as the constitution is followed.

The Democracy was developed in Greece 500 years BC and is used as the form of governance in most western countries and in more and more countries around the world.

In the spirit of democracy, we must, with the freedom of governance that it is meant to give us, make decisions.

We are free to decide which party to vote for, which means that we support the idea that we are all in principle equal, a form of governing intended to give freedom, but which takes all people under one comb. In other words, having as a manifesto that everyone in principle is equal and consequently should share the benefits of society.

No problems with that side of democracy. If this form of governance, as practiced by some socialistic parties in Europe, had the prerequisite to work, I think even I would sympathize with it.

There is only one small problem with sharing the wealth, and it is first and foremost: where does it come from and who created it?

Then, what about sharing the many negative consequences that occur when the wealth suddenly doesn't exist anymore? The cash has run out because of low motivation, general downturns, or lack of incentives created for the creative powers.

Most importantly, in my opinion, is to find the answer to: Where did the wealth come from and who created it?

What percentage of the population believe that economy means that there exist buckets full of money which could be shared between us all? Maybe simply phrased, as fortunately, fewer, and fewer believing it's like that.

Moreover, unfortunately there are many meanings, and often with justification, that some manage to get much more than others. Probably correct, corruption happens everywhere and not least here in Spain.

As far as I understand, Spain is topping the list in Europe in this context, but in all fairness, they're working hard to get to the bottom of it. But, as with all ingrained habits, it takes time to get rid of them.

Greed is indubitably a bad thing and of course there are many in society who, without social responsibility, abuse their position to enrich themselves. It is unfortunately a natural consequence of human nature and proves that we are in no way equal.

In nature no animal would survive if it wasn't the strongest and best in the tribe that became leaders. A democracy in the animal world would probably lead to extinction.

Maybe we would be wise to dwell more about that?

If everyone is to decide, presumably the only justified form of governance, society will slowly but surely stop if one doesn't open for compromises. It must be acceptable that some are better than others to create, and that they, under responsibility, must be given stimulating and motivating conditions. Many democratic societies fortunately has understood this.

In today's democracies, individuals can decide which political segment they want to belong to. In this way one obtains affiliation and has a platform from where to express opinions, and thus achieves a social safety.

How many political segments, or parties, a democracy might consist of is determined by the citizens of the democracy. Anyone is free to form one's own political party. If one reaches the given minimum votes, one is in progress.

It is morally correct that no one, "without consequences", should enrich themselves on the expense of others. Just the little "without consequences" is the most important thing, because it is unfortunately in many people's nature to try and let the morals sail in its own sea.

Are leaders with the ability to fill the buckets, equally good at leading the community? Without arguing for or against, I believe that's not the case. Protecting wings spread throughout society, and the considerations that must be taken to ensure all, do not belong to those making every effort to achieve financial success.

Possessing diplomatic skills and having studied all the rules and regulations of bureaucracy, does not give any guaranty for you being a good leader and far from you having financial flair. In this context the black and white rule does not necessarily apply.

Speaking of contradictions and accepting that it is so, it is only logical to accept that both extremes are necessary conditions for the community to function. Both extremes must be stimulated to do their best.

Tolerance, balance, and compromise are important factors in this context.

Regarding the politicians, I go along with Nelson Mandela's

definition: Politicians want their ideas to stay alive.

The more people deciding, the more bureaucrats are needed to investigate and clarify all different views. Bureaucracy is costly and the bigger it becomes the more complex and expensive it gets. By the very nature, bureaucracy itself creates a continuous need for growth within its own ranks.

It is hard to imagine a democracy that would work without bureaucracy. Considering all the fractions in society, the term: "The more chefs the more mess", comes to mind.

Wikipedia describes the bureaucracy as follows: "Bureaucracy is a hierarchical organization of decision making where individual cases are handled by caseworkers with carefully defined decision-making authority by common rules and where all employees' "bureaucrats" are responsible to management for decisions to be in accordance with the regulations. The purpose of bureaucracy is to ensure equal treatment of similar issues and a high level of detail control from management.

Bureaucratic organizational form is a prerequisite function for public administration in a democracy to work, but one also finds traits of bureaucratic organization in (larger) private companies. Emphasis on the correct procedure often leads to a bureaucratic organizational form, among other things, being criticized for spending unnecessary time deciding. Therefore, the word "bureaucracy" in the daily language is usually used as a derogatory expression of cumbersome case processing."

The Irishman Edmund Burke wrote about conservatism in a democracy back in the seventeenth century:

"I believe in the essential weakness and corruptibility of human nature, in the incapacity of the average man to resolve his problems in a rational manner, in the irrelevance of most "rational" solutions to political problems".

According to Burke, the community is not a rationally constructed structure, but an organism that develops gradually.

Any attempt at radical turmoil must therefore end in disaster. The constraints of reason make it important to respect traditions and fear revolutions.

Wikipedia describes Establishment as a denomination of the dominant group or elite that holds power or authority in a nation or organization. It may be a socially closed group that chooses its own members or specific elite structures in a government or a specific institution.

Political bureaucracy also includes an elite governing and dominating.

To me precisely because, as described in Wikipedia: "The Establishment" is a designation of a dominant group or elite that holds power or authority in a nation or organization, it can easily get a protectionist side.

Would it not be natural that those who work in "The Establishment", seek protection by sheltering themselves from the insight of us deadly? In their eyes, we are likely to be narrow-minded and to incompetent to understand the complex overall picture that concerns the governance of society.

The more complicated and comprehensive, the more shielded and insensitive becomes "The Establishment". Purpose achieved.

Should democracy work after the definition, "The Establishment" and its bureaucracy must be made visible, accessible and attackable in one way or another.

I don't have an answer to how it can be done in a peaceful way, but I have no doubt that it is necessary.

June 2024

The ninth of June 2024, in Spain, was probably the major political breakthrough in the last few years for those who have chosen the Partido Popular, or Conservative Party, as their political preference.

The election, which was held in each of the 27 countries affiliated to the European Union, chose the policy that will lead the European Community in the years to come. The same election will of course also have the greatest significance for the respective countries.

In Spain, where I have now lived permanently for twenty years, the result of the election showed that here, in line with most other countries in Europe, it was a breakthrough for the conservative form of governance, the Partido Popular, and a general decline for the socialists. But, and I see this as a big challenge going forward: In the wake of the conservatives' progress, there followed, at least for me, a not unexpected progress for the so-called ultra-conservative groups. This was especially true in France and Italy, where they dominated, but progress was also marked in several other countries.

In my book "In the spirit of Democracy", which will be published in the beginning of next year, I will include this small report, which perhaps underpins some of my thoughts and attitudes regarding today's politics.

In the book, it also becomes clear that it is precisely this development that I thought had to come.

For a long time, in my opinion, enlightened people could not help but see that this had to happen.

The current practice of socialism in many countries is, in my opinion, based on what I interpret as one of many aspects of Extreme Democracy and which I briefly allow myself to describe as follows:

"A political form of governance where ordinary average citizens' common sense of what is right and what is wrong when it comes to attitudes to justice is disregarded.
A form of governance where minority groups with strongly deviating attitudes to the average all too easily get their views heard and where those in power, to maintain the political balance, act extremely tolerant and often disregard constitutional considerations".

This means that most ordinary citizens with common sense feel that the relation to law, respect, order, and not least tolerance, have gone far too far. There are no limits to the consideration of minority groups' perception of what should be accepted as normal.

Many "healthy" people's perceptions are thrown into disarray, and not least, it becomes difficult for the younger generation, who are the ones who will stand for the future, to relate to norms and rules. The latter is not least thanks to the parents' lack of firm attitudes, which is, among other things, a result of how they have been influenced over time by those in charge. Where the Socialists have been responsible for the management of society, in my opinion they have in many cases made themselves responsible for ultra-radical groups gaining a greater foothold.

Hopefully, seen with my eyes, this means that a large and dominant group of normal conservative forces will also see a big advance.

Spain
George Manus

CONTENT

MY 84 FOOD FOR THOUGHT ON POLITICS

DEMOCRACY II
Democracy the way it's practiced these days, brings us slowly but surely against major challenges.

July 2019

LET THE MASSES RULE
My opinion is that if you let The Masses Rule, as was the case during the French Revolution from 1789 to 1799, the world will come to a standstill. As a consequence, those who work to make that happen may become responsible for the dissolution of our society.

2017

OBJECTIVITY AND DIPLOMACY
Let us appear a little more Objective – just a little more Diplomatic – only a few times a week. We don't need to stretch ourselves more to make the world a better place to live.

POWER OF EXAMPLE IN POLITICS I
The good will win by the Power of the Example. The real decline begins the day you lose the sight of this reality.

March 1992

REVOLUTION
Revolution in politics often strikes a negative cord – while the Revolution associated with technical development gets applause.

DIPLOMACY
"I have a great understanding for your opinion, but...."
2010

ENDEAVOUR
Making society more transparent is one of the most important ingredients in creating understanding and respect between humans. At the same time everything must be done to make the machinery of society more straight-forward for those of us who for different reasons don't spend the most important part of our life trying to understand the complexity of today's governance.
2018

POLITICAL BUREAUCRACY II
Bureaucracy is a brake-pad in the modern society.
2018

POLITICAL BUREAUCRACY I

The more people involved in deciding, the more Bureaucrats are needed to clarify the different views. The Bureaucracy cost and the bigger it gets the more complex and expensive it becomes. By the very Nature, Bureaucracy itself creates a continuous need for growth.

June 2016

SIMPLIFICATION IN POLITICS

The trick is to Simplify without impairment.

April 2019

THREAT IN THE DEMOCRACY

Allowing all "ideological extremes" in the world to express themselves in social media results in uncontrollable and irreparable situations. Democracy gives, as far as I understand, no precise definition of "ideological extremes", so this challenge cannot be solved. In dictatorial societies, this is naturally no problem.
One of the challenges of Democracy is therefore to find solutions that do not discriminate against "ideological extremes" when it comes to adapting freedom of speech, a privilege we all should have.

February 2019

EXTREME DEMOCRACY I

Those who support the Extreme Democracy will one day understand that they thereby have undermined the fundamental values of Democracy.

May 2019

BICKERING

If I could write music, I would have composed a wonderful accompaniment to the Bickering and endless interruptions one witness during the Spanish political debates before the election on April 28th.

April 2019

EXTREME DEMOCRACY II

The extreme Democracy is created by the myth that we all are alike. If we don't stop this development, all forms for ultra-radical organizations will flourish.

May 2019

EXTREME DEMOCRACY III

The Extreme Democracy is, after my opinion, as destructive and dangerous to our society as any kind of left or right-wing Extreme organization. The Extreme Democracy is responsible for forming the breeding ground for increased influence of radical left and right-wings.

May 2019

EXTREME DEMOCRACY IV

Extreme Democracy should be defined and made available as a form of governance in line with ultra-conservative or revolutionary socialistic form of governance.

May 2019

EXTREME DEMOCRACY V

The best example, seen with my eyes, of Extreme Democracy in practice, is the Spanish National Assembly's treatment of amnesty for the several hundred involved in the illegal elections in October 2024, on Catalan independence.

POLITICAL EVOLUTION

Evolution means development over time. In countries not yet having found a reasonably good balance between socialism and conservative-ism, and there are many of them, it is natural that other extremes occasionally are voted in to help to govern. This happens for the development not to go too quick for people to adapt. The road to a balanced, just world society is long – very long – infinitely long.

May 2019

POWER OF EXAMPLE IN POLITICS II

A new political party should be called the Power of Example. The only way the Democracy will be respected, is that its leaders represent the Power of Example. Everyone not understanding that should stick to other forms of political governance.

May 2019

ON DEMOCRACY I

It is difficult to imagine a Democratic form of governance that can operate without bureaucracy. The more cooks the more mess, is an expression to refer to when considering all fractions in society.

2016

POLITICAL NEGOTIATIONS

*Is there anything pompous about Negotiations?
Negotiations are nothing more than communication between parties, with intent to end up with some kind of agreement. When
Successful Negotiations don't lead to results, it is often due to lack of
understanding and respect for the opposing party's arguments.*

May 2019

ON DEMOCRACY II

*When we talk about contradictions and accept that they are always
there, it is only logical that one accepts that extremes are necessary
for society to function. Everyone must therefore be stimulated to
give their best. Tolerance, balance and compromise are important
factors in this context.*

2016

DEVELOPMENT III

*Development cannot happen without sacrifice. Those who believe
that the world can continue through stagnation must be naive.*

2016

ON DEMOCRACY III

*How many political segments, or parties, a Democracy should con-
sist of is determined by the citizens of the Democracy. Everybody
stands free to form their own political party. If only you reach the
necessary minimum of voters, you are in the process.*

2016

ON DEMOCRACY V

In nature, no animal would survive if it were not the strongest and best in the herd that became leaders. A Democracy in the animal world is likely to quickly lead to annihilation. Maybe it would be wise to think a little more about it.

2016

DISCRIMINATION IN POLITICS II

Some people should never have power in politics — but who should judge in our democracies?

Sept. 2019

ON DEMOCRACY IV

Is it not natural that some of those who work in the political establishment do what they can to secure one another by shielding themselves from the insight of us ordinary mortals? In their eyes, we are likely to be too bigoted and incompetent to understand the complexity of the wider picture that concerns the governance of society. The more complex and comprehensive, the more shielded and unapproachable the establishment becomes. Purpose achieved. If Democracy is to function according to its definition, the establishment and the bureaucracy must be made visible and attachable.

CORRUPTION II

Corruption is society's worst poison and unfortunately has no political boundaries. The power of example's will always be among the strongest.

Oct. 2019

EXTREMISM

Ruling politicians in our democracies are all responsible for the Extremism's uprising. They beg on their knees for them to promote themselves by acting much to permissive in their policies.

July 2019

STOP THE WORLD

Brexit leads to isolation –
Isolation leads to weakness -
Weakness leads to stagnation -
Stagnation leads to retrogression -
Retrogression leads to power concentration -
Power concentration leads to survival of the fittest -
Survival of the fittest leads to lack of social benefits -
Lack of social benefits leads to poverty and revolts.
Then it starts all over again related to isolation.

Sept. 2019

POLITICAL ISOLATION

As Isolated, you will always find partners, the question is just whether it will eventually end in new collaborative coalitions. This, however, will in turn lead to revaluation with other coalitions. There is only one way forward and that is collaboration.

Sept. 2019

ELECTION

It's a saying that: "Some vote with their brain and other with their hart". This was probably the case in the Spanish Election on November 10. 2019, so we can only blame ourselves for getting what we get.

Nov.. 2019

TRUST POLICY

Trust Policy can only work through the power of example. The only way to maintain respect for democracy, is that it represents leaders showing power of examples. When the power of examples shows its right face as well in business as in political life, a sustainable management is established.

May 2019

ONE WORLD

Is democracy a temporary security valve? Reason suggests that it's impossible to allow all individuals to determine the development of society. Perhaps nature has been instrumental in deciding that we need an incredibly long development time to reach the final solution: One World, every-ones world.

May 2019

OPPONENTS OF DEVELOPMENT

In demonstrations we hear that: "Capitalism kills the world". For our world to survive, money is required. In my opinion, money is created through capitalism, and should of course be taxed sensibly. Thereafter the funds should be managed by the Governing politicians. If capitalism is strangled, many of us will face tight conditions.

Sept. 2019

A PLACE TO LIVE

I definitively did not settle in Southern Spain because of the country's politics, but because it's a wonderful Place to Live as a pensioner, despite of its politics.

Nov. 2019

SOCIALISM AND CAPITALISM

Socialism and Capitalism are result of experience. Socialists believe, and perhaps rightly, that Capitalists aim is to suppress and exploit those in society that do not represent the elite, while the Capitalists, also perhaps rightly, think that the Socialists use most of their time and efforts to get rid of them. Who can balance these extremes?

Sept. 2019

POLICY AND INTERACTION

One definition of Politics is that Interaction between the state and the rest of the society happens. It must mean that Politicians will always remain, whether the cooperation is good or bad.

Oct. 2019

CORRUPTION III

It is said that opportunity makes thief. Does that mean Corruption is happening because of existing opportunities?
If so, it is difficult to come to terms with the Corruption in any other way than blocking the opportunities? Can that be done in accordance with the ideals of democracy and human rights?

Oct. 2019

REGARDLESS

No matter how democratically one organizes society, there will always be an "elite" who governs. Should the "elite" be the ones who understand and respect the responsibility they have, or those who only argue that they will take care of and protect all the citizens of the society.

Dec. 2019

LOSERS AND FANATICS

*Expression of Democratic opinions should, after my opinion always
be respected, but remember, after my opinion again, there are basically only Losers or fanatics who walks in front of political demonstrations about power in society.*

Oct. 2019

IS IT NOT STRANGE?

*In transparent democratic elections, the winning party represents
the politic to be followed. Strangely, the same people who voted for
the winner rarely get satisfied with their policy implementation.*

Nov. 2019

PENSIONERS AND SOCIAL SECURITY

*Future Pensioners and people on Social Security can only hope that
today's governing politicians give those who create momentum living conditions that stimulate efforts, so that the result of their activity through taxation provides the financial basis to keep everyone in
society going.*

Nov. 2019

FINANCIAL DEPENDENCE

*Financial Dependence between countries is a major factor in
avoiding serious conflicts.*

Nov. 2019

THE FUTURE AND WORKPLACES
In the Future, it will not be the matter of finding Work for every-one. The challenge will be that everyone must be given a meaning-ful existence.

Nov. 2019

LACK OF ADAPTATION
As long as there is no understanding of dependence on each other, the words Lack of Adaptation is what slows progress for all of us. Some professions will have to give way to change. Logically, this will lead to protests and challenges, but nothing can change the natural evolution. Politicians must learn to use the word Adapta-tion and put it to life. If not, we continue to waste valuable time fighting for a hopeless future.

2016

TODAY'S DEMOCRACY IN PRACTICE
I'll love an omelet, but please don't break the eggs.

POLICE AND PROOF
Something is wrong when the Police need photographs to prove their conduct during demonstrations with clear violations of demo-cratic rights.

Oct. 2019

POLITICAL OPPOSITION - COUNTERWEIGHT

Opposition and Counterweight is necessary. It is only when extremism comes into the picture that everything comes into imbalance.

Dec. 1019

UNITY AND SEPARATION

In my opinion, every human being understands that Unity is the way forward. Make it abundantly clear to yourself that those who believe that separation is the future are called SEPARATISTS.

Oct. 2019

FORWARD AND RETRACTION

It is not always the case that a move Forward is the right one. Strategic Retraction can sometimes be important for the final progress.

Oct. 2019

EVERYONE FIGHT FOR OWN IDEAS

In politics Everyone is Fighting for Own Ideas. Nothing wrong with that, but if everyone Fights like that there will be no common denominator, which is a prerequisite for progress.

Nov. 2019

PROGRESS AND RETROGRESSION
Progress is easy to promise, but challenging to create - while Retro-
gressions come by them-self if you don't fight for Progress.

2016

SPAIN'S POLITICAL COALITION II
My feeling is that the Spanish coalition government is a virus in
addition to the Covid 19. It has proved very difficult for them to
treat two viruses at the same time.

April 2020

ABOUT SETTING BORDERS
Setting clear boundaries does not always mean that they Are locked.
Through diplomacy you often find compromise.

Oct. 2019

POLITICAL DILEMMA
The art for modern politicians is to pacify the small percentage of
the population that destroys the possibilities for democratic flourish-
ing. But that's not democratic, is it?

Oct. 2019

PROGRESSION OR STAGNATION

Either way, if the wheels are to continue rolling, it's only one way and it's going forward. Turning time back is catastrophic, especially for those thinking it's better to take a bigger part from the wealthy. Money only exists if it's created.

POLARIZATION

The strange thing is that Polarization happens both when extremes are approaching each other - and when parties distance themselves.

Oct. 2019

VIOLENT POLITICAL DEMONSTRATION

Removing the first 25 meters of a Violent Political Demonstration, one can, from the reaction of the remaining, get a solid basis to judge its real intentions.

Oct. 2019

HOW IS IT POSSIBLE?

What kind of a government has a democratic country that cannot keep track of its inhabitants? The rules, of course, state that if you go outside the law, you are punished. How can things then happen as they do in Spain these days?

(With reference to the 2017 Catalan independence referendum)

Oct. 2019

ECONOMY

A non-moving Economy means standstill, and standstill means decline. As in everything else, without decline and rise there will also be no progress.

Nov. 2019

TRAGIC RESULTS

Seen with my eyes, the result of the Spanish election and the coalition established between the PSOE (Labour Party) and PODEMOS (Camouflaged Communist Party), if it last over time, be Ruin - Oppression and Republic.

Nov. 2019

CHANGING TIMES

There are things which in the past seemed disgusting, which today are acceptable, and things today we think are disgusting which one day will be fully acceptable.

Jan. 2020

FUTURE AND PAST

Significant leaders understand the importance of the Past. They realize there is no Future without a Past.

April 2020

PUT ON THE TIP?

Statistics in Spain show about the same number of unemployed as one year ago. The country has mostly been closed since early this year due to the Corona virus. Artificial breathing from the state to avoid many bankruptcies is not included in the statistics, which would otherwise show huge increases. The politicians portray the development as not being so negative?

April-May 2020

THE NEW NORMALITY

Spanish Prime Minister Pedro Sanchez boasts that he has intro-duced the phrase "La nueva normalidad."
Let's hope that no one uses this phrase for anything other than the Covid 19 epidemic.

July 2020

DEMOCRACY III

Democracy's weakness is that honesty is suppressed. (One avoids calling a spade a spade).

August 2022

SPANISH POLITICS

After my opinion Spain is undoubtedly a Klondike when it comes to democracy. Controlled by a coalition between socialists and communists, the information is governed as if it were intended for children.

March 2021

DEMOCRACY V

Feel free to call it democracy, but if you let everyone decide, there can only be one way and it is not pleasant to think about.

Jan 2020

DEMOCRACY IV

One thing is for sure, seen through my eyes. I'm going to go to the grave as a disillusioned man when it comes to the results of democracy the way it's practiced these days.

February 2021

HUMAN RIGHTS

Human rights must be limited to the rules the humans themselves have helped to shape, through fair elections.

April 2021

LEGAL – ILLEGAL

What is Legal and what is Illegal is interpreted as different as there are numbers of people on earth. The written laws of the various countries are probably respected to a greater or lesser degree, but the morally dependent unwritten ones it's worse with. We can only assume that most of the humanity is law-abiding.

June 2019

TWISTED

With so many Twisted people as it is in the world, it would make sense to be more critical when choosing those who are elected to govern and care for us.

July 2019

POPULISM

The art for the Populist wanting to rule, is to mislead people to vote for her or his policy by all possible means, false or true.

March 2019

MORALITY

It is Morally incorrect that someone, without consequences, should be able to enrich themselves at the expense of others. Precisely the little "without consequences" is most important, for it is probably unfortunately in the nature of many people to try and forget about Morality.

2016

CULTURES MEET

Most people want a world that is best for most people, but since the road to achieving the goal is seen from every one's own Prospectives, it is doubtful whether one will ever reach it. The only thing that is certain is that it will take longer time than anyone is able to understand.

June 2019

FREEDOM OF EXPRESSION

Freedom of Expression should be obvious in an enlightened world, but unfortunately it isn't. But even where Freedom of Expression is working, it doesn't mean that because one has an opinion about a subject, one must always express it, going to extremes and fighting on the barricades for same.

April 2014

DIPLOMATIC ABILITIES

Even if you have Diplomatic Abilities and have studied laws and regulations of bureaucracy, this does not mean that you are a good leader and far from you having financial flair. Here, as otherwise often, the black and white rule doesn't apply.

2016

STIMULATING WORKING CONDITIONS

If everyone is to decide, presumably the only justified form of governance, society will slowly but surely stop if one doesn't open for compromises. It must be accepted that some are better than others to create, and that they under responsibility, must be given stimulation and motivating conditions. Many democratic societies has fortunately understood that.

UNITED STATES PRESIDENT

That 78 million voted for Donald Trump should be a wake-up call for democracy to change its style. Today's democracy, at least as it is practiced in Spain, in my opinion encourages extremism.

November 2020

ABOUT DEMOCRACY VI

The more people who are to be involved in deciding, the more bureaucrats are needed to map out the different points of view. Bureaucracy costs money and the larger it becomes, the more complex and expensive it becomes. The bureaucracy itself creates a continuous need for growth.

2016

THE POWER OF THE POLITICIAN

The politician's strength should not be judged by his manner of speaking, but by his way of being and his way of showing power of example.

THE POWER OF EXAMPLE III

Nothing can stand against the good and the power of example.

January 2021

SPAIN'S POLITICAL COALITION I

The Spanish coalition government is in my opinion a virus in itself. When the time comes, they will have to pay its price.

April 2020

MY REFLECTIONS OF LIFE VALUES AND ATTITUDES

No order of priority

AMBITIONS AND THE SUB-GOAL

April 2013

Not everyone possesses a competitive spirit. This, among other things, is what ambition stands for, "the desire to compete, aspiration".

It all has to do with yourself. As with prestige, it is something personal. But it does not necessarily have the same negative connotations as prestige in my opinion.

"The desire to compete, aspiration", In this context I don't see it as being in competition with others. I choose, at least for the time being, to look at wanting to compete as something you want to do for yourself, compete with yourself and whatever ambitions you might have in each situation.

Here the driving force comes into it again. Where there's no driving force, it's difficult to find progress.

Of course, lots of people are happy without having ambitions. Why do so many people see being without ambition as something negative? Imagine what the world would be like if everyone had limitless ambitions?

I think we all agree that not everyone can be academically inclined. What about the countless number of service jobs needed to get the world to function? It shouldn't, in any way, mean that someone is worth less or lacks ambitions just because they aren't academically inclined.

Society ought to function in such a way, that those who have personal ambitions should basically be able to achieve them.

Sporting ambitions, if they only concern yourself, are both necessary and correct to have. If your ambition is to reach the top, then many self-denials and sacrifices are necessary; if you aren't motivated and don't have steel-clad ambitions, you simply won't reach your goal.

It is worse when parents have ambitions on behalf of their children.

I begin with some personal experiences from my early days in business.

Before I turned twenty at the end of the fifties, I was already responsible for the training of approximately 40 technicians.

Even then, I noticed that many of those who already had families fought hard to give their children an education, as they felt they themselves had not been able to have one due to the war.

It was a matter of course, that if it hadn't been for the war, they would all have done their A-levels, gone to university, and ended up with important positions.

Following the war, children without the necessary abilities were practically forced to get an education they weren't suited for, and often ended up with big problems. Many family tragedies unfolded because of the often well-meaning but misguided ambitions parents had on behalf of their children.

The worst examples of this – the sports ambitions of parents for their children – I personally witnessed later.

I was reminded of this the other day, during a conversation with our local golf pro.

The golf club had just finished a golfing event organized by the Spanish Golf Federation with participants of both genders, in the so- called "Juvenile" class, from 8 to 16.

He just shook his head in despair at how he had seen various examples of over ambitious parents dominating these children and youngsters during practice, resulting in both tears and the gnashing of teeth.

My own examples are similar when it comes to both tennis and skiing, and from the time when my daughters were growing up and were, of course, members of the local clubs for these sporting activities.

This was in Oslo in Norway and took place on the so- called better west-side where we lived.

You could at times witness literally horrific incidents. I even had to cancel my daughters' memberships at the local tennis club due to its over ambitious leadership. The example is too grotesque to mention, as it didn't directly involve my daughters.

It was not uncommon to see parents who, during simple slalom competitions, threw themselves out onto the slope when one of their hopefuls fell, with an outburst of excuses that they had wrongly waxed the skis, or that the fall had been caused by badly sharpened steel edges.

That you want to see your descendants be successful is obviously human, but with this type of ambition it back- fires all too often.

I have included a reflection called: The sub-goal, related to my own sporting ambitions in golf, which I wrote in August 1995. I call it the sub-goal because my intuition tells me that it'll become a sub-goal, even though it has been the main goal up until now.

The happy day, the 9th of August 1995. The goal which seemed impossible to achieve, has been reached.

Oh well, it probably never seemed impossible to achieve; but there's no doubt of it having been high up and a long way away before being reached.

I've just got home from the golf course, Bogstad. It's close to half past nine in the evening and the obligatory bath has been carried out.

Now I'm wandering quietly around the dining-room table with a towel around my waist, in an eternal circle, Pocket Memo in hand.

Totally relaxed and with a wonderful feeling in my body.

"Single figure handicap".

The goal has finally been reached. The number 9, not two numbers, just the one. How in the world can it be that something so insane as a tiny number, can be of such importance in this context? Only to yourself, of course.

Just two simple little strokes separate me from my previous handicap, which was 11 – just two strokes. Whether they're 200 metres or 30 centimetres is of no importance, the fact is that we're only talking about 2 strokes in 18 holes.

Ideally speaking 18 holes should normally be completed in 72 strokes, with a minimal variation depending on the difficulty of each course.

I have opened a bottle of red wine and lit the two candles on the table. I'm waiting for the chicken to heat up. The rice is almost ready and in one or two minutes I'll let the peace flow through me.

It was a fantastic round. Impossible for a non-golfer to comprehend, but when I think of having played the course in 77 strokes, five over par for the course, I can barely believe it's true.

It all happened in a Thursday match under perfect conditions, where I, with my 11-handicap, played to 42 Stableford points.

Now I understand once again what it means, what the meaning of the thesis I so often use is, namely that: "It's not the goal that's important, it's the process that counts".

Now I've reached my goal, but I realize that from this moment on, it has become a sub-goal. "Single figure handicap", I will from this day look upon as a sub-goal and not the goal itself, and as just one of the many steps in the stairway. That's how it is. How many steps the stairway has is unimportant. Figuratively speaking, it could be an infinite number.

The thought of what my next sub-goal in golf should be, is unclear.

Will I ever be able to repeat the result or, better put, improve it?

It's great to realize that a goal becomes a sub-goal when it's been reached.

***

MY FOOD FOR THOUGHT ON
AMBITIONS AND SUB-GOAL

AMBITION
The desire to be successful in your chosen field.
Ambition, requires a lot of renunciation and sacrifice.
If you are not motivated and single-minded,
you may never reach the goal.

2013

THE TARGET
Hitting a Target does not necessarily mean that you have used a
weapon.

2015

FOCUS AND VISION
Focusing on the goal is most important of all - while Vision is need-
ed to check that all conditions are in place to reach it.

GOAL
The closer you get to the Goal the more important the details be-
come.

May 2019

COMMUNICATION AND THE VOICE

April 2013

Communication is largely what you want it to be.

As the communication I'm thinking of here is verbal, I have in this reflection included part of my Reflection "The Voice" from 1995.

In my opinion, the best definition of communication is: "the process which has the unit of thought as its aim" from Wikipedia.

There are many definitions, of course. Just think of how versatile communication is, regardless of context.

As mentioned before, I'm married to Marianne who is Swiss. In May we will have been married for fifteen years and while my Spanish is quite limited, she speaks it fluently. I don't speak French, which is her mother tongue. We have always, between the two of us communicated in English.

Even though I'm a British citizen, I've been based in Norway all my life and have thus only my Norwegian school English as a starting point; and there wasn't a lot of regular school.

Regardless, it's a great combination. Even though you normally become more tolerant and understanding towards your marital partner as the years go by, very few believe me when I say that in these nearly fifteen years we have never come close to having what I would describe as an argument. The answer lies, among other things, in having as a safety net the fact that you are not communicating in your mother tongue. "I must have misunderstood what you meant".

This immediately shows your tolerance, but also affords the better half the possibility of smoothing things over by saying: "Yes, I realise that you must have misunderstood. What I really meant was…"

Is this communication? Regardless, no one will feel defeated or lose their pride; aren't we lucky?

I hope no one takes me too literally in this; it's probably not all that simple.

I don't think a poor foundation can be fixed this way. Communication has, as mentioned, an infinite range. The voice itself used for verbal expression is decidedly the most convenient form of communication, and it is here, in my opinion, that the perfection of the voice shows itself.

A word, a sentence, with different intonations, is interpreted differently. This happens when you can't see the person you are talking to. Joy, sorrow, expectation, and questions, all expressed in a combination of phraseology and intonation.

The intonation expresses, often better than the words themselves a particular state of mind.

In connection with an earlier reflection – the one that I wrote about the smile, I included both the voice and the eyes, because I wondered whether the smile could stand on its own, or if it had to be seen together with, for instance, the voice and the eyes.

In that context I felt that it was natural to ask the question; but regarding the voice, it can hold its own and it does so quite often.

Not least every time you are calling someone. Depending on the nature of the conversation, your voice changes intuitively according to the messages you want to convey.

Answer words, expressed in different ways, can give you anything from the strongest fear to the purest joy.

This divine instrument can play on a never-ending number

of strings.

Even animals are very sensitive to this instrument. No one believes that they understand the language that's being spoken to them. No, they react, of course, to the voice as such.

We are perhaps not conscious enough of the way we use our voice, or is that precisely what we are? Shouldn't you always, and especially when speaking on the telephone, consciously think about how your voice is interpreted by the person you are talking to? It becomes especially important perhaps, when it has to do with people who are closely connected to one another, and where subtle nuances are significant.

The further you are apart, geographically speaking, the more importance I feel you should give to this.

The voice is also a significant weapon and very versatile when used as such.

The funny thing is that precisely when used as a weapon, the voice is perhaps the best of its kind; but, unlike others, it can have its greatest effect when not being used.

Is there something called "silenced to death"?

The voice can both love and hate, but we mustn't let ourselves be misled into thinking that it operates on its own.

Some people speak without thinking, of course, but that's not what I mean.

No, the voice will forever remain an instrument and, as such, is controlled by the brain.

My personal experience with communication over the years has been all enveloping, in the sense that I, as an employer, had close contact with employees on all levels and of both sexes. Only rarely, as far as I recall, was it necessary to admit to a failure of communication.

I didn't always live up to the policy of my firm. Each employee should have the full right to know as much about the running of the firm, so that even if they didn't always agree with its decisions and objectives, they should, if interested, be able to understand the motives behind them.

It obviously didn't sound quite like that in the company policy, which I wrote at the time, but this part has unfortunately been lost somewhere along the way.

These days such ideals may sound totally misplaced in the business world, and attitudes like these probably find little acceptance in today's personnel management.

In a family context, my experiences as regards to communication, especially in my younger days, was a little different. I was at times accused of being a coward when I didn't enter what were, in my opinion, one-way arguments, the outcome of which had already been decided before any communication had begun.

There's something in the saying that "where there is nothing, even the emperor has lost his rights".

Fortunately, these situations were few and far between, but they have stuck in my mind.

Distortion of the truth or a totally one-sided attitude make communication difficult, if not impossible, and the same goes for unwarranted accusations. Desperation builds and that's when you see compromise or giving up as the only solution.

Many will probably draw the conclusion here that I can't have been easy to get on with, and I can sympathise with this view. I don't know if my personal experiences have left scars that are too deep, but the wounds have not been easy to heal.

I hasten to say that I have an excellent relationship with

most people I know, so in that context I'm talking about water under the bridge.

If a partnership is based on a solid foundation, it should, in most cases, be possible to come to an agreement through communication based on compromise.

***

MY FOOD FOR THOUGHT ON COMMUNICATION AND THE VOICE

COMMUNICATION I

*The ideal form of Communication is the one
that even those without preconception can use and enjoy.*

1989

COMMUNICATION II

*You improve understanding by recognizing that details and shades
are needed for a balanced Communication.*

October 2013

COMMUNICATION – BELIEFS

*One of the reasons why Communication becomes complicated is that
everyone is right based on their beliefs.*

2018

TALKATIVE AND LISTENER

*As Talkative everything goes out while little comes in.
As a good Listener everything comes in,
while only that which is of value to the person stays there.
The combination of being Talkative and at the same time a good
Listener is an art form.*

Sept. 2019

COMPROMISE

March 2013

Everyone has a clear idea of what the word compromise means.

Making compromises in our daily lives is quite common for most of us. We don't normally give it much thought, nor do we look at compromise as being a sacrifice. I give a little here, the other party gives a little there, then we make a compromise having given way equally, without either party having got things exactly his or her way.

Is it really that simple?

I would like to believe that the simplest form of compromise is the one that produces no consequences other than personal sacrifice. By that I mean that no other than the parties involved should personally suffer from the consequences the compromise demanded. That can be serious enough, but in any case, you have full control over the consequences and can judge for yourself whether others will be harmed.

It becomes more complicated when someone enters an act of compromise on behalf of others. Here, the consequences can be very serious, so the person who has authorised the compromise to be entered into, should have done thorough research about the consequences this could have.

It can be even more challenging with compromises that are made, where the consequences can be of a completely different dimension. For example, when countries make trade agreements between themselves, or things like that. In such cases, it is usually delegations from the parties who negotiate until a compromise is reached. The consequences will probably not normally be directly personal, but may have other far-reaching consequences.

The above mentioned consequences of compromises are fortunately not something you normally think about in the daily life and hopefully it is the case that some of us enter compromises without thinking too much about the consequences, and that is good.

It is precisely those small daily compromises that you should get used to making to maintain balance in life, as they have an inestimable importance for your own self-satisfaction.

When travelling around, you find places where, in certain situations, all trade is based on bargaining. The seller starts with prices that are sky-high, the idea being that these will be brought down to a level, which both parties are happy with. This is also a form of compromise, but in my opinion a somewhat misguided one. Here there is no equal distribution of giving. The seller's contribution, the reduction in price, has been put in as a calculating factor. He knows where to draw the line, in other words, the lowest acceptable price, which still gives him a reasonable profit. The buyer on his or her part should also be aware of the situation and close the deal only if he or she finds the price acceptable.

Am I in the wrong here?

I'm far from happy with this procedure, regardless of the cultures practising it.

If I must compromise, however, perhaps it isn't so bad after all?

Is it only because I'm generally not happy with this type of procedure that I don't like it?

Many of you probably feel that this is just the right form for trade, as here one can argue and negotiate and influence the outcome.

At least that's what you think, but those of us who are a bit wiser, know that it, the price that is, has already been decided beforehand: it's the seller who decides.

Those who share my attitude normally pay too much, to the seller's delight. In other words, you ought to stay away from this type of trade if you aren't familiar with bargaining. Some love it. They feel great when they can let loose in a situation like this and that's good for them.

Now, let's get back to compromise, which is the result of negotiations where none of the parties gets things 100% as they want them, but are still happy.

I mentioned that there is no sacrifice in this form of compromise, and I believe that; but let's look at the kind of compromise where the distribution of benefits is in no way equal, where one of the parties feels that he or she has given a lot more than the other one but goes along with it in any case. This can be tiring after a while.

That it happens occasionally can't be avoided and it usually works both ways, but when the scales keep tipping in one direction it can become difficult.

My original name, before I was given the surname, Manus, by my stepfather Max on my eighteenth birthday, was George Hans Bernardes. George after my English father and Hans because my mother felt there should be something Norwegian in my name. (Hans isn't just the name of a king of Norway from 1483 to 1513, like George in England, but also a family name from Ulvik in Hardanger.)

Here there was probably also a compromise, as I was given the name Manus, but was never adopted.

***

MY FOOD FOR THOUGHT ON COMPROMISE

COMPROMISE I

*Compromise is probably one of the most important words we have,
apart from love.*

2017

COMPROMISE II

*If the parties are not completely out of balance, Compromise should
be possible to reach.*

2013

COMPROMISE III

*The ability to compromise is something we must all learn,
but whatever you do, don't let it become a permanent state.*

April 2019

COMPROMISE AND HONESTY

*There is no point in Compromising Honesty,
as it's only a question of time before disclosure comes with unexpected and usually unpleasant consequences.*

April 2014

CONSCIENCE

January 2001

Let me point out straight away that this is a very sensitive subject.

Conscience is probably one of the most flexible concepts there are, as it always involves morals as well as judgement and feelings.

Everyone bases their conscience on their own judgement and ethics, thus emphasizing its flexibility. In my book "Thoughts", the first 51 days of 2001, I wrote among other things about conscience:

"I suppose conscience is something we are all concerned about. Whether it be good conscience or bad, it will always be there as part of our daily life. Then there is something about suppressing a bad conscience and the pleasant feeling you get from a good one. It may have to do with important things or just silly little things, but it is always on your conscience."

At that time, I meant it the way I wrote it, that everyone in one way or another is concerned about their conscience. Now, almost 12 years later, I've revised things a bit as you will see later, when I state that many seem not to have any conscience at all.

We have laws, of course, which, in our democracies at least, are meant to be guidelines for how we are to behave in practically all situations. They are there for our own good according to those who have written them, but even though this is largely correct, I think most of us feel that we are swamped with laws and regulations and that many of them can only be understood by a selected few.

Everyday rules and regulations are fine, for example those

concerning traffic. Here it's a question of saving lives and reducing damages.

Every one of us decides how the state's rules are to be followed based on judgement and conscience.

After many years' experiences of driving in Spain, my judgement is usually based on the theory that, despite the speed limit of 40, most people drive between 60 and 80. The motorway limit of 120 means a minimum of 130 and is often closer to 150, with many exceptions over 170.

The stop signs mean, to a lot of people, just go if the road is free.

Especially for most of the locals in small towns, one-way signs mean: "Just drive if no one is coming against you and you can get quickly to your destination".

A widespread sport for those who normally drive at 150 on the motorway, is to see how close you can get to the car in front without making physical contact.

I must admit though that a greater respect is shown at pedestrian crossings.

It's no longer a sport to see how close to the pedestrians one can get without hitting them.

Most things are improving after all.

All examples seem to be based more on judgement than conscience.

According to their own judgement everyone acts correctly.

So far it was all about judgement, but where does conscience enter the picture?

Lots of people probably have no conscience at all, so they just drive around in their own world. While many probably have a conscience but it's buried and doesn't surface until an accident has happened and it's too late.

For whom or for what should you have a conscience in traffic?

I don't want to be seen as a saint in this case, because I'm not, but let's look at drinking and driving for instance. In this I'm quite consistent and I can confirm that, since I was 20 years old and until I first came to Spain about 15 or 20 years ago, there was seldom, if ever, a question of having a single glass when the car was my mode of transport. Things did change to a certain degree upon arriving in Spain, where a glass or two with meals followed by a brandy with one's coffee, didn't stop anyone from driving home.

Having a morning coffee in the local bar, you often saw the local police with their *carajillos* (coffee with a dash of brandy) at the start of their working day. I think I became quite conscious of what I was doing, drove more carefully and did not suffer from a bad conscience, but I would be telling a lie if I said that, at the beginning and until the late nineties when I was here only on sporadic visits, I kept to my Norwegian habits.

Gradually, as the rules were sharpened here as well, with regular controls, everything changed. Today the combination of drinking and driving has become unthinkable for most people and that's as it should be.

I don't know whether it has to do with my conscience or my moral responsibility not to hurt others, but if it has to do with both so much better, I now choose total abstinence when driving.

Perhaps most of it does have to do with the tiny good or bad consciences. The big ones are probably so overwhelming

that if you have a conscience to begin with, you try "the ostrich game". To put your head in the sand and pretend you
aren't there.

Has anyone tried to examine or count their good and bad
consciences? I wonder if anyone could come up with some
sort of norm, showing the percentage which would bring you
within acceptable limits.

It would probably be too complicated, however, and your
conscience shouldn't be left to others, as it is clearly among
your most personal possessions.

I have at least one bad conscience, which I don't want to
share with anyone until one day I've left it behind.

The more I think about all this, the more I must admit that
I too, to some extent, participate in "the ostrich game" in this
context.

Conscience, judgement, and morals belong together. Of all
the proverbs I've seen about the conscience, this Persian one is
the finest:

"The zest for life comes from a clear conscience".

***

MY FOOD FOR THOUGHT ON CONSCIENCE

CONSCIENCE I

Nothing is better than the feeling of a clear Conscience.

CONSCIENCE II

If you believe you made a bad decision that had an adverse effect on someone or something, then your "Conscience" is not clear on that act.
However, it can be clear on other decisions you have made.

November 2012

CONSCIENCE III

Whether it concerns a good or bad Conscience, it is always with us as part of our daily life.

2023

GOOD AND BAD CONSCIENCE

Everyone is acquainted with both Good and Bad Conscience - while the degree of the good or the bad is essential to our well-being.

DEPENDENCE

December 2013

In some form or other we are, I believe, always and throughout all stages of life dependent on someone or something. From the time we see the light of day for the first time, we are dependent.

No sooner has the umbilical cord been cut, we are normally at the mercy of the person we have been dependent on throughout the entire pregnancy. The big difference is that now others can move in and help take over some responsibility for our further development.

Regardless, we are still at the mercy of and dependent on someone else.

No matter where in the world we happen to be born, and under whatever circumstances, rich or poor, those who think money makes one independent are terribly mistaken; we are always dependent.

Can you make yourself independent from dependence? Only by extreme manoeuvres I would think. But do you really want to?

Dependence is quite natural, has a completely natural place in your everyday life.

We are always learning something, whether it be part of your formal school education or not.

Also, when you get out into the real world after school, it is always a question of learning something.

The day you give up and says enough is enough, there's no point in learning anymore, that's really the beginning of the end.

Regardless of how you look at it, you are dependent on others to learn.

It is said that he or she is self-taught. The basis of being self-taught must start with something you have learnt and thus, if you look at it in isolation, it is probably more a case of indirectly building on the experiences of others, which reveals us dependent again.

Dependence as a challenge faces many people who for various reasons need others around them to exist.

I can imagine, even if it isn't part of my own experience, that most people in such a situation will do their utmost to become independent.

Unfortunately, certain situations often make this impossible; you are just, and always will be, dependent on others.

The above examples relate to human dependence. What about the more distant dependences, those most of us don't think about too much in our daily lives?

For those of us who are lucky enough to be growing up in the so-called modern world, it is natural for both clean water and electricity to always be present. We take it for granted and complain about the smallest inconvenience, caused by a power failure or having no water for a few hours when a pipe has sprung a leak. Here we have entered material dependence, and this comes in many guises. We, the spoiled ones, take too many things for granted; after all, we pay for them through our taxes, don't we?

On the screen, appeals are made to put aside a few kroner a month for those millions of people who don't know what clean water looks like, and who barely encounter electricity in their everyday lives. Some people must go along with these requests, or we wouldn't see such campaigns on TV.

There are pictures of children drinking water with which we wouldn't even mix cement, and they must walk for hours every day to get to water sources for these precious drops. Regardless of your social level, dependence exists.

We have also become totally dependent on mobiles and the internet, as well as an ocean of other gadgets, and we feel like the world is coming to an end when occasional irregularities occur with these. We obviously are happy to be dependent.

Indeed, we insist on it in our everyday lives, by always aspiring to the newest and latest gimmicks. This, of course, doesn't apply to everyone but clearly to most of us.

Another form of dependence, and one which can be more serious for the person or people concerned, is the dependence which can affect your health, or which often destroys family life. Here you must be careful, as I believe there are several factors playing a part. Each one must think about themselves and their own lives. Otherwise, within the extent of time and interest, everyone can choose to involve themselves in organizations they believe may have a positive influence when fighting dependence and abuse.

I have fortunately never got to know any form of what I, from lack of knowledge, lump together under the heading "drugs".

From the age of seventeen to twenty-three I smoked cigarettes. The reason I quit over night was that, throughout adolescence, I had a constant struggle with my tonsils. Finally, the day came when I was called in for an operation to have them removed. My innate fear of everything to do with hospitals and white coats spurred me into action. The hospital visit was cancelled, and my last cigarette extinguished.

The fear must have remained in my subconscious, however, because until the last couple of decades I have at times had very unpleasant experiences with tonsillitis but have never again smoked.

Alcohol is a different story. Despite a steady trickle of red wine throughout the years, from the time I first discovered this gift of Bacchus – during my two-year stay in Italy at the age of seventeen and eighteen – until today I can honestly say that there have been no negative side-effects. Since the first days of my youth, I have never had what one might call a hangover, or to my knowledge any other adverse effects. The volume has stayed steady and at the same level for the last fifty years.

When my daughters grew up, we constantly heard about tragedies happening due to the association with certain types of "substances". I believe I chose the easiest way out by making it clear to them that, regardless of how much I loved them, I would help them with anything else, but if they got involved with "drugs" they would be on their own. I believed then and I still do, that this is something everyone must deal with on their own. When you have got into this vicious circle, you can only get out of it on your own. I am humble and tolerant when it comes to other points of view in this matter, but am happy that we, as a family, have been spared this - at least as far as I know.

Since I have never been a gambler, I also don't know anything about this dependence, except what I might read about the problems which may befall both families and people who are unable to moderate themselves in this context. Again, it's a question of your personal balance and control over the danger of becoming dependent. It seldom effects your health if a balance exists, but there is no doubt that many families have broken up as a result, and that related tragedies take place every day.

To use but not abuse, in other words to find the golden middle way in all of life's challenges, is what you ought to strive for; but never forget that you must also live the one and only life you have been given on earth to the full.

***

MY FOOD FOR THOUGHT ON
DEPENDENCE

DEPENDENCE I
*If you have a special attitude to another person,
you should expect that she or he has a special attitude to you.*

June 2018

DEPENDENCE II
*Is it not, in some way, a sense of security in the fact that we Depend
on each other?*

Oct 2019

DEPENDENT AND INDEPENDENT
*It is not a defeat to be Dependent - as long as you do everything you
can to become Independent of what makes life miserable.*

2018

DEPENDENCE III
*No matter where in the world we happen to be born, and under
whatever circumstances, we are terribly mistaken;
we are always dependent.*

2013

EXPERIENCE

October 2013

There is something pretentious about the word experience. "Experience suggests that".

As a general expression, you normally let it pass without closer reflection, but if it is connected to serious speeches presented by people in authority, you ought to listen carefully.

Where would we be without the lessons experience teaches?

Wouldn't we just be repeating our actions, whether the repetitions are justified or not?

How often would we be correct in our repetition? In our everyday life we are not consciously aware of the way we use our experience. For most of us, we automatically draw our own conclusions. We base our actions on our experiences and subconsciously make minor or major adjustments.

As a result, it is one of the main factors which help us develop throughout our entire life. It would be very sad if, at some point, we told ourselves that that's sufficient experience, let's flick the switch.

In a way it would be the same as putting your hands in the air saying, I've got nothing more to learn, there's no point to the learning process.

Those people who consciously acquire knowledge until the very end are the happiest.

It is of course also true that theoretical knowledge builds experience, though not immediately in a practical way.

Is there also something called spiritual experience, which complements practical experience?

Through schools and universities, you get an academic education. The experiences you have gained because of your studies are, of course, both valuable and necessary, you hope, when it comes to applying for a job. But even when your career choice isn't of a practical kind, but of a more academic type, the question of experience is always raised.

You stand there with your exam results and are treated the same as all the other applicants. Regardless of who gets the position and the criteria used, you can ask yourself who should cover the costs to get the experience, which must be gained to do the job properly.

It's most likely the employer who must invest to benefit fully from their employees' education, and that is probably as it should be. Naturally enough, you can't be equipped for the task you are given before you have gained the right experience.

A different situation involves education of a more basic character, which needs to be combined with business practice within a chosen profession. This combination of schooling and practical experience is, in my opinion, by far the best when it comes to career choices. I hope it still exists in some form or other.

When I started working at the end of the fifties, we had several apprentices employed in our firm. They were to reach their journeyman or trade examinations.

They were normally employed in the service department, had apprenticeship contracts and, if I remember correctly, were given two days a week off to attend the vocational school to get a theoretical education.

As far as I can understand, this arrangement has been replaced with other versions, but I'm not up to date on this.

The question is if the apprenticeship scheme, in a more modernized form than the one we had back then, wouldn't be better and more interesting for many of those who feel the need to get into a craft early on, rather than fight their way through a higher theoretical education in which they have little or no interest.

I have heard that the apprenticeship scheme is practised successfully in Switzerland, for instance, and that in England there are constant references to the fact that more apprenticeships ought to be created.

I take this as a sign that this form of education is still considered the best when it comes to practical training.

I greatly believe in a working environment involving a combination of theoretical and practical training.

I have often heard said, "If only others could learn from our hard-earned experiences, how much better everything would be." That way of thinking is both short-sighted and meaningless in my opinion. You must be the master of your own experiences; I'll go so far as to say that it is only through your own experiences that you can progress. Here I exclude obvious well-accepted experience based on investigation and science. Such experience belongs to all theoretical education on all levels, and automatically provides a positive benefit in most cases.

In this context knowledge can be drawn from other people's experiences.

Not that you ought to believe that all experience is worthwhile; and I don't think anyone does. Everyone has, in one form or other, suffered a bad experience.

The conclusion is that it isn't important if your experiences are good or bad, if you learn from them.

Bad experiences don't trigger repeats, while the good ones ought to do so.

I believe it would be good for us all to focus more on the value of experience.

Think about the experiences you have benefited from in life, especially where you believe they have been important for your development. Then become more conscious of them.

Most of us are, I believe, equipped with a good or not so good ability to suppress bad experiences. I call this ability a safety valve. We can't keep filling up with too much negativity, especially as regards the bad experiences we suffer from at times.

We ought to suppress some memories of them, when we feel that it's necessary, to maintain an acceptable balance.

I believe that the best experiences that have contributed to my development, I gained during my time at school in Italy in the late nineteen fifties.

***

MY FOOD FOR THOUGHT ON
EXPERIENCE

EXPERIENCE I

*Bad Experiences do not trigger repetition - while the good ones
should inspire them.
It may be good for all of us to focus more on Experiences.
Think about what Experiences you have had throughout your life,
of the kind that you think have been of importance to your development, then raise your awareness of them.*

October 2013

EXPERIENCE II

*Not all Experiences are of the good kind, but they are part of our
lives and thus help shape our personality.*

Dec. 2019

EXPERIENCE AND KNOWLEDGE

*Experience is something you gain over time
- while Knowledge is a result of Experience.*

EXPERIENCES

It's unwise to underestimate Experiences.

2013

HONESTY

It is high time I grabbed hold of "honesty" and finally come to terms with this, for me, painful subject.

Ever since I started working, I have been immensely irritated by the expression, "to be honest", or its other variation, "in all honesty". Not only has it irritated me all these years, but at times it also made me furious, because I cannot imagine a more idiotic expression, within the contexts in which it is normally used.

How can you trust someone using these kinds of phrases? What the person in question is saying is that, normally I'm a totally dishonest person, but in this situation I will make an exception, namely to be honest. Stuff and nonsense.

Now, of course, there will be many reading this who, if being honest with themselves, will realize that they them- selves use this expression. To you I have only got one thing to say, and that is: stop using it this very instant.

Next time you hear someone expressing him- or herself, listen carefully. You will be surprised at how much dishonesty you will observe.

Of course, you can say that this does not mean much within the greater context, as it is only a matter of an expression. There's no way I personally can take that attitude.

While I am on the subject, it feels natural to add the expression: "Truth be told". What on earth is the meaning of that? Should the truth not normally be in the forefront? Does it mean that you are not normally trustworthy, not expressing the truth? Is the truth to be saved and only brought forth at special events or occasions?

In my opinion, if that's the case, the world has become un-
hinged.

A typical old-man's expression you might say. Very well, but
if that is your attitude it means that you are either indifferent
to the above-mentioned approach, or you accept it.

Don't forget that another generation is coming after us.
What are they going to believe and think if we don't give them
guidelines?

Again, the excuse of many will be these are just clichés. I
regret this attitude is too prolific in our daily communication.
Most of us, I think, will fight for the freedom of speech and
the right to express ourselves. In the spirit of democracy, we
want it that way.

Some Danes have made cartoons offending the Prophet
Mohammed, while a video recently produced also seems to
offend those who worship the Prophet, and who have him as
their guide in life. Retaliations, riots, and killings have been
the result of it all.

We live in a world which allows us insight into whatever we
want. The whole world is open to us if we are interested. How
many religions and communities do we have on this planet?
Furthermore, how many sects and special varieties do we have
who represent different opinions of how life should be lived
and what it should consist of.

At the end of the day, the questions will be and have probably always been the same: who is the strongest, who will win
and what means will they use to win, or at least advance in the
hierarchy of preferred religions and their splinter groups?

However, "being honest", I think that every one of us
should be able to live as we wish and make the best out of our

life on earth, based on our own assumptions, but that is when I am "being honest".

This last statement has probably got its weaknesses. What would I mean in this context if I were to be dishonest? If I had skipped the first "to be honest", I think my basic attitude would be crystal clear.

Summary: I think that every one of us should be able to live as we wish and make the best out of our life on earth, based on our own assumptions.

***

MY FOOD FOR THOUGHT ON
HONESTY

HONEST FEELINGS
Respect peoples' Honest Feelings - and treat them gently.

HONESTY I
Honesty has no competitors.

HONESTY II
Honesty is also not to be despised.
Suspicion and jealousy are poison and can be hidden dangers on the
road of life. If you make Honesty part of your daily agenda,
as well as a good portion of tolerance and respect for one another,
many of life's sharp edges can be rounded.

From a wedding speech in 2005

HONESTY AND LIES
If you Focus on Honesty and give it full support - Lies will retreat
without a fight.

INSPIRATION

July 1994

A strange word – where does it come from? The word that is? Latin, of course – explained as: empathy, inhaling, perception, enthusiasm, divine impulse. In my translation it is like receiving something.

Well, where do you get inspiration from? Are we all given inspiration or is it granted too only a select few?

Regardless, we all need inspiration from time to time; or don't we?

In my opinion, inspiration is something which you can, to a certain extent, create.

You can't just sit there and wait for the inspiration to come. You must, as for instance in marketing, conduct outreach surveys to achieve results. The orders don't just come strolling along on their own.

Inspiration to do what, or for what?

We're used to artists needing inspiration to perform; we've sort of grown up with that.

I heard the other day that Grieg composed some of his best works in a tiny cabin in Utne. He apparently found valuable inspiration there. I don't believe the inspiration just came to him, he probably sought it out, just there in those scenic surroundings. His composer's hut, the little house down by the water, a stone's throw from the main house in Bergen, we've all heard about.

The Norwegian painter Thaulow's unique rendering of flowing water: inspiration?

He apparently spent a lot of time "on sight" in the cold. Inspiration costs.

Is inspiration synonymous with creativity? It's easy to say

that something successful consists of 10% inspiration and 90 % perspiration.

Quite possibly, and in my case the perspiration percentage could be increased to 99.

Regardless, we must admit that inspiration is a necessary factor, that little or nothing can be created without inspiration but, once again, where does it come from?

For some, it perhaps comes in the form of a revelation: eureka. In this context I find it natural to bring in our inborn curiosity as an element. Not the normal kind of curiosity, where you stick your nose into other people's business, but the kind of curiosity which consists of wanting to know what's hidden around the next corner.

You appear with an open mind, you are receptive, nothing enters a closed hand, as we know.

It's like with a funnel; the wider the opening the more goes through. If you bare that in mind you can, in a way gather the ingredients, or put differently collect the seeds which will germinate.

Perhaps that is inspiration.

The best form of inspiration probably comes from other people. In this case it's not a question of blind worship of people with authority and power.

We're not all the same. There are people with a special-radiance and power who don't abuse it.

Why was he or she inspiring to talk to? Why was it an inspiring meeting?

If you let yourself drift along, let yourself get immersed in?

Is it when that happens that you get inspiration?

All in all, I feel that life itself is the most important inspiration.

MY FOOD FOR THOUGHT ON
INSPIRATION

INSPIRATION AND ASPIRATION

Inspiration to create something is an essential ingredient for Aspiration - which is the desire to attain or achieve something you do not have, or become something that you want to be.

INSPIRATION I

Life itself is the most important Inspiration.

1994

INSPIRATION II

You can't just sit there and wait for the Inspiration to come. For instance, in marketing you must conduct outreach surveys in order to achieve results. The orders don't normally just come strolling by on their own.

July 1994

INSPIRATION III

If You have an open mind, you're receptive; nothing enters a closed mind, as we know. It's like a funnel: the wider the opening the more goes through.
If you bear that in mind you can, in a way collect the ingredients, or put differently, collect the seeds that germinate.

2023

OPENNESS

April 1994

In my opinion we humans are not very open.

Some might think they are, but they're not - deep down. That we are calculating in most of what we do - goes against openness.

We only find genuine openness in nature, where calculations don't form the basis for anything at all.

Notice for instance how flowers attract the bees. The petals willingly let go of the heart of the flower, to make room for the bee - that's genuine openness.

I have two valves - one main valve located deep inside is often closed - and the other - the outer one - controls the flow from the inner to the outer valve. I'm lucky to have the outer circuit.

To those who don't know me, I probably seem open - I'm not.

I think most of us have at least two valves. It's important, very important, that you can protect yourself like the fox, having several exits from your den.

Openness can turn back on itself. Tell all and you become vulnerable.

It's better to let openness come in doses - study the reaction. Is it real?

Uncertainty - doesn't it come from a lack of openness?

What's it like in the animal kingdom? I can't imagine a cow in a field holding something back to achieve something specific.

Although, does a dog which is begging show openness? Hardly - it has just learnt from experience that by begging it will achieve something.

It's probably not human nature to be open. Were we like that originally, and have we just learnt not to be that way?

Is there more openness in primitive societies? In my opinion it would be logical if it were so.

We live in a closed society, it is said. Does that term mean that we don't let others in or at least only to a very small degree?

If idleness is the root of all evil - could openness, then be the root of all good?

See to it that you don't become too open; it may be good to hold something back - just in case your openness is abused.

***

MY FOOD FOR THOUGHT ON
OPENNESS

EXPOSURE
Is it only stupid people who expose themselves, or is it a symbol of security and honesty?

April 2020

LISTEN TO THE WORLD
Listen to the World. Digest what you hear, make use of what you find valuable and make the best out of the situation.

June 2019

TRANSPARENCY AND UNCERTAINTY
Uncertainty is often the result of a lack of transparency.

2019

TRANSPARENCY AND NATURE
True Transparency can only be found in nature, it has no limitations. There are no restrictions on anything.

2017

PATIENCE

January 2019

"I'll be right there".

It usually starts with an agreement that something is going to take place at a specific time, but which for unknown reasons is being delayed.

Both parties are ready, and a time is confirmed between themselves. Then, for some reason, one of them got hindered and thereby delayed. The one who, according to the agreement, expects that the thing that should happen will happen, in other words the one not causing the delay, will normally, from the time the agreement was made, start the countdown by showing patience.

This is where each of us shows our quality of being patient or lacking it. What makes most of us tend to lose patience at some point, is when a delay that is more than expected takes place.

Is it the time we lose that we see as valuable, or is it the shortcoming of expectations? The agreement is made, and the expectations are thereby unconsciously built up, only for them to be pushed forward in time.

Is patience a human phenomenon? Animals, especially domestic animals such as dogs and cats, do not seem to have the same problems with patience as we humans, at least not the question of patience that has to do with time. Is it because their assessment of time is different from ours, or that their instinctual expectations are different?

Dogs, which I have most experience with, especially English setters, certainly do not lack expectations. They, who otherwise appear to be devoid of this property in their daily lives are quite clear when the hunting season is on. Then they reveal expectations to the fullest. Whether it's experience because they are used for hunting or if it's inherited instincts, I do not know; but I have many examples that show that they possess strong expectations and that there is no way they can control their **impatience**.

When I think about it, it's far from correct that dogs appear to be devoid of patience in their daily lives. Just look at the tail movement of the dog when you retrieve the dog lead, or when you are on your way to performing another of the dog's daily positive routines. The dog's patience does not turn into irritation if the action fails to take place; but, when that happens, you can clearly read the disappointment resulting from the failed expectations, in the dog's body language.

Not all types of patience have something to do with time.

Take, for example, the patience that is related to things where you compromise daily. Here too patience can be put to the test. Different kinds of bad habits, or repetitive patterns of action that you are not totally excited in others, are not always solved by allowing it to lead to criticism, which then becomes the subject of hurtful discussions. No, instead you allow tolerance to lubricate your patience.

This model can often be used successfully over short periods of time, but if you compromise by using tolerance and patience over too long a time, it can harm your health.

Another thing is that the possible expectation that the cause of the bad habit, or the repeated annoying pattern of action will disappear by itself, is something you will rarely or never experience.

If we could all be a little more conscious when it comes to giving others reasons to put their patience to the test, much in everyday life would be easier.

MY FOOD FOR THOUGHT ON
PATIENCE

PATIENCE II
*Unfortunately, Patience is often exploited and rarely gets any other
thanks than the good feeling of helping others.*

PATIENT AND IMPATIENT
*As Patient you wait with a smile - while as Impatient you get upset
and stressed.*

January 2019

PATIENCE AND EXPECTATIONS I
Patience becomes less, the greater the Expectations you have.

January 2019

PATIENCE AND EXPECTATIONS II
*If we could all be a little more conscious about not giving other rea-
sons to test their Patience, much in everyday life would be better.*

January 2019

PRESTIGE

April 2013

Here it is a matter of your own reputation and then it becomes both personal and difficult. It is unfortunately so that what becomes personal can easily develop into becoming uncomfortable. It is a protected world, where others have no right to be; or have they?

For some, prestige has no meaning in their daily lives, whereas for others it is vital and counts every hour of the day, all year round.

It is this prestige I'd like to dwell on a bit. I've experienced various sides of it, but I must admit that my experiences haven't always been positive. Not that they have been important to me, but I have found people concerned with prestige to be navigating in their own world. If they themselves are aware of this it must be their own decision, but perhaps prestige acts as a protective shell, something you can hide behind in order not to be too transparent? Perhaps its prestige which makes them function and gives them purpose in their everyday life?

The most important aspect is not what they themselves represent, but what they believe they represent to those around them. The strange thing is that if they don't come across as people who share their values, then they pull out their entire arsenal, as it becomes important for them to leave a prestige-filled impression. Is it done to impress or, once again, is it to hide something?

There is often no limit to what others offer by way of conversation, and certain pet topics are frequently repeated. I've thought about whether there is something deeper behind this.

Is it the case that people who seem to have experienced

most things in life, feel that it's still important to give the impression that they have done even more than they really have? Is it a built-in inadequacy or perhaps an additional need to hide something, which must be satisfied?

Up until now, it has all been about verbal prestige, but that's only one of its facets. Expressions like, "that lends prestige to the person in question" or, "that's a prestigious position" speak for themselves and carry no judgements.

Used in such contexts, there are no negative thoughts behind them.

What about the type of prestige, which has to do with trends and status?

Trends are normally something which concerns the younger generation, and though they are seldom so far along in life that prestige - the way I see it - has taken root in their consciousness.

Young people just want whatever it is because others have it, and because it's trendy. This is rightly called peer pressure.

I've got a bit of a problem seeing the difference between prestige and status, but I am sure there is a difference. The struggle for social status, for instance, has more to do with living up to other people's standards, and the wish not to be different.

Status symbol is the name given to that which you acquire outwardly, in the form of prestigious cars, boats, etc. This type of prestige goes deep with a lot of people.

I remember well, when my then common-law wife, who a year later became my lawfully wedded wife, got her first Hyundai Coupé in 1997. She bought it on my recommendation. I had been around to Oslo's car dealerships with my son-in-law, to have a look at their selection. I don't remember the name of the dealership, but we noticed a car I thought looked very stylish in the car park outside. It turned out to be a Hyundai Coupé which belonged to the sales manager and was the only one at the time of its kind to have been imported. I talked to my wife in Spain on the phone that same afternoon and she started her local enquiries immediately.

By chance she heard that a car dealership in the town, Cuevas del Almanzora, half an hour's drive from where we lived, had become a Hyundai agent. She ordered the car unseen and had it delivered after a fortnight.

My surprise was great when she met me at the airport with her newly acquired car after my visit to Norway. She hadn't mentioned anything to me about the purchase.

My wife has since had two further cars of the Coupé type and changed just a few months ago to a smaller model, the i30. I have had two Hyundai Santa Fe's. The last one I had for seven years, and we can't express how happy we are and have been with all of them. I'm not being paid by Hyundai for these superlatives, even though it might seem so.

I won't mention what brand of car I'm currently driving, as it might upset my idea of prestige.

So where does prestige enter it?

Well, it took several years before you could talk openly about the Hyundai brand in Norway. You also didn't see many of them on the roads and there definitely wasn't any prestige or status involved in driving this brand. In fact, for some it was rather embarrassing. Prestige and status meant driving Audi, Mercedes and BMW; only then did you belong.

Eventually more Santa Fes were being used as taxis, and today we probably talk about both KIA and Hyundai as drivable vehicles; but there's no prestige in driving either of them, as I understand – at least not in Norway.

No, the similarity or difference between prestige and status, I can't seem to come to grips with, so I'll try to stick with pure prestige.

I can't help mentioning an example, which must have gone quite deep. A friend of mine, an employer, once told me of a work problem.

In a difficult economic period lay-offs became necessary. A particular person holding a high position, had for years performed impeccably for the firm, but finally the day of his redundancy had arrived. The person in question – who understood the reason behind the lay-offs, offered to take a drastic drop in salary or to change his position internally, but insisted his title must be kept.

I'm inclined to draw the conclusion that it must have been his social status, as well as prestige, which caused this reaction.

Here we go again, prestige and status.

Something more down to earth: in 2002 the biggest oil spill in the history of Spain, Portugal and France took place. Hundreds if not thousands of kilometres of beaches were destroyed, when an enormous tanker broke in half and went down on the Spanish north-west coast. The name of the tanker was "Prestige" and it spilled 63,000 tons of oil.

In my thinking, prestige doesn't guarantee anything at all.

***

MY FOOD FOR THOUGHT ON
PRESTIGE

PRESTIGE

Prestige gives no guarantee whatsoever. The tanker "Prestige" went down in 2002 and 63.000 tons of oil leaked out.

2013

PRESTIGIOUS AND TOUCHY

A Prestigious person can often appear Touchy.

January 2019

POMPOUS I

Do some people appear Pompous to cover an inferiority complex?

May 2019

POMPOUS II

Feel pity with those who believe that respect increases with their Pompous behaviour. I believe most people's opinion is the opposite.

Nov. 2019

PRIDE

May 2014

"It's nothing to be proud of", or the opposite, "I'm proud of you", or: "You can be proud of that", are expressions you pay attention to, particularly if they come from someone with authority in one area or another and applies to yourself.

It's something about being careful before contacting someone with the expression, "It's nothing to be proud of". You should in advance have a thoughtful reason for doing so. Nothing is more hurtful than if the accusation for using the expression is incorrect and only based on assumptions and rumours.

If someone says, "It's nothing to be proud of" to you, think carefully before you answer.

Maybe the right thing to do is to test yourself every now and then. How would I react if someone told me that, "It's nothing to be proud of"?

If someone address you with the expression, "I'm proud of you", and you know it's well meant, then you feel the warmth.

Being honest, which, of course, you are, never use the expression "I am proud of you" for anyone, unless you mean it full heartedly.

We know it is warming when someone uses that expression with us and we know it is well meant and deserved.

However, if you feel that it's not honestly meant, or maybe it's somewhat sarcastic, it can sear quite strongly.

Maybe you should tidy up your own use of these types of compliments.

How often do you yourself use the expression, "I'm proud of you"?

Think about how you would react if you were to hear these five words from someone who means a lot to you; wouldn't it warm you?

Pride shines out of the eyes of the person concerned; the purpose is achieved.

The goal has been reached. The bigger the offer has been and the more you have sacrificed to reach the goal, the prouder you are.

I think we have all been acquainted with the good feeling of pride.

This type of pride is just as big whatever the case. It's not a matter of the size of the feat. Everything is personal and proportional.

Whether the first time you balanced on a bike, the distinction you got in sport or other milestones, the pride is personal and proportional to the efforts you made to reach the goal.

The most important type of pride is the one on behalf of others. It gives double pleasure, especially if you have personally been part of that which the person in question deserves the expression for. "You can be proud of that".

We all have a hint of personal pride, and that's both right and important.

When this type of pride gets overdeveloped, however, it becomes difficult to deal with.

With an overdeveloped personality it feels good to express that one is proud of what one has done.

It's often the way the pride is expressed which matters. "Modesty is a virtue" is an expression.

Do you act with a superior attitude because you are afraid of making a fool of yourself, or of exposing yourself? Has it something to do with taking yourself too seriously?

Personal pride should not be overdeveloped.

In my opinion, the most sympathetic pride is the one shown on behalf of others – but it must be honest.

***

MY FOOD FOR THOUGHT ON
PRIDE

PRIDE
The Pride you have on behalf of others is the best form of Pride.

2014

PRIDE AND ARROGANCE
*If people looked more closely at how the encyclopaedia describes
Pride and Arrogance and left these burdensome traits behind, many
would be perceived as far more sympathetic.*

February 2019

PRIDE I
Your personal Pride should not be overdeveloped.

2020

PRIDE II
*Little can hurt more than if someone tells you:
"That's nothing to be proud of ".*

2023

SELF-ASSESSMENT AND SELF-CRITICISM

December 2018

Could it be possible that this topic came to me completely by itself, or was it triggered by something very special?

It doesn't matter. It's a typical example of something that has been lying and smouldering, which the subconscious has quietly worked with over time.

Tolerance has, of course, been put to the test for a long time, and all forms of compromise available have also been nurtured.

If I don't immediately mention that a case or an opinion at least has two sides, or parties, and that I am conscious about it, anyone could say that this isn't an objective opinion, but a clearly subjective assessment.

Admittedly, when I feel pressured, I am not the easiest, but at least I have a willingness to try to build bridges.

The way we look at ourselves or judge ourselves may vary quite considerably, as we are all different.

Nevertheless, the main feature is that we generally add better qualities to ourselves; that we think we are a little better than we really are, and that we have a clearer view of most things than most others.

Here it sprinkles with the fertilizer for self-preservation. What about self-criticism? Clearly, most of us think we are self-critical. We generally don't like to be criticized, but if we criticize ourselves, it stays only between ourselves and our own conscience.

No one gets to know where we really stand. There's a lot of good protection in that, and you are not so easily exposed. Many find themselves in such a world. In that way, they shield themselves from the outside, believing that everything is fine and green, and for them it is so. They often remain in their own world, find their place in the hierarchy and function perfectly in the whole.

There are areas where I think it's appropriate to exercise some self-criticism, however, and that is related to behaviour in everyday life. Ask yourself if you are a person who usually takes others into account?

Think about it carefully. It's not a matter of covering a big field. From the moment you start the day to when you go to bed, you encounter an infinity of situations where you deliberately or unconsciously leave an imprint of your personality.

You are judged by others based on your actions and behaviour. If your attitude is that you do not care, then you can't expect anything but general negativity towards your personality.

In this context, it's amazing how important the real smile is.

A smile costs nothing but gives so much. Yes, I claim that it requires very little from your side to be perceived as a considerate human being.

Not that you should in any way expect someone to give you this in writing; but the most valuable gain you're guaranteed to get is your own good feeling of knowing that you are generally a considerate human being.

Now, don't let this go to your head. You will have many negative feelings if you're not perceived as how you want to be; but it's not your problem if you are otherwise satisfied with the sincere attempts you have made to act more considerately in daily life.

***

MY FOOD FOR THOUGHT ON
SELF-ASSESSMENT AND SELF-CRITICISM

SELF-ASSESSMENT-SELF-CRITICISM

*The best way to become a better person is honest Self-Assessment
checked through Self-Criticism.*

December 2010

SELF-CONSCIOUSNESS

Being Self-Conscious is in no way the same as being egoistic.

May 2019

SELF-CONSCIOUS

*None of us can help being the way we are, but it probably becomes
easier, in many contexts, if we are a little more self-conscious.*

SELF - PRESERVATION

*In general, we believe we have better qualities than we have, that we
are a little bit better than we are, and that we have a clearer view
than most others. "The older we get the better we are."*

December 2018

STUBBORNNESS

May 2012

I won't immediately characterize stubbornness as a disease in line with what I believe extreme jealousy to be. Here as elsewhere there are many degrees and nuances.

The simple, well-known form of stubbornness, which everyone has and at times applies, is of a relatively innocent character.

In fact, it can be both humorous and charming and is part of everyone's daily life and relationships.

We can also skip lightly over the kind of stubbornness children use to attract attention. That's a gift of nature and a prerequisite for development. It's not in any way damaging but has, of course, a strong impact on the child's upbringing. If the cry is honoured repeatedly to achieve family peace, it suggests that you are doing the wrong thing; so it's clear here as elsewhere that you must find a balance. Maybe in the long run family peace is more important?

As we know, black and white is not always a workable alternative. Perhaps it seems the simplest, but it is in no way the most character building.

We can probably all agree on what has been said so far: you must add a bit of spice to everyday life in order to make things work.

It is worse when someone's stubbornness becomes a kind of obsession, turning towards the fanatical. Against all odds and common sense, and with a total lack of logic and sense of reality, a lot of people forge ahead without considering the turbulence they're causing when dealing with others who, within the given context, react normally and use these very senses to navigate through the waters of everyday life. It is especially bad for people with a strong sense of fairness. Everything turns upside down when normal values are set aside by such brutal and illogical means.

The result is unfortunately quite often a temporary break in communication or worse.

Total resignation is felt by the affected party, while the initiator, with his or her extreme variety of stubbornness, moves on through life as if nothing has happened.

You must ask yourself if it's possible for someone to be so removed from reality that they have no idea of what they've started. Or could it be that they feel that it's a means, with a bit of luck, to achieving changes in conditions, things, or situations?

Both are probably adequate reasons.

Wouldn't it be easy for those affected to think, oh well, this is so crazy that we'll just let it go, take it all with a smile and defuse the situation?

Those who recognize themselves will probably say that they have, of course, tried it that way, but that there are limits to how far you can stretch when the situation repeats itself several times in a row over a long period of time.

Those who have managed to read this far probably ask themselves if the writer of these words can refer to his own frightening examples of stubbornness, and I can assure you he can.

***

MY FOOD FOR THOUGHT ON
STUBBORNNESS

STUBBORNNESS
Anyone who doesn't give up always finds a solution.
Maybe not the right one, but anyway. Any solution gives freedom.

May 2019

STUBBORNNESS I
The worst Stubbornness is that which for some becomes too great an
obsession, a turn towards the fanatical.

2016

STUBBORNNESS II
Stubbornness can easily lead to communication breakdowns and
worse.

2019

STUBBORNNESS III
Some use Stubbornness to change conditions, things, or situations.

2020

TOLERANCE

2017

First, to be very plain about the word tolerance: it means to withstand and hold out, not physical strength. "Tolerance is the ability to withstand living with those who have different opinions and attitudes and who then acts; in other words, those which you do not usually accept".

This should be a reflection for all of us.

Most of us will add something more direct to being tolerant, something more to the point. Either you tolerate this or that, or you don't.

Seen from that angle we clearly speak of something black or white or what?

That is not the case.

The description of tolerance states that we are talking about a balancing act.

You tolerate to a greater or lesser extent, which I consider is good.

In other words, I claim for a fact that tolerance is not black or white.

Tolerance is a balancing act and Compromise is the weight on the scale making it balance.

Compromise must be part of the balancing act.

It is impossible to perform a balancing act without adding the ingredient of give and take, in other words, Compromise, and that I think is good.

Imagine how well those who mean they are tolerant feel. Such an attitude becomes subjective, as others undoubtedly may have a divergent view.

Standing a little further away, a little more on the outside, pretending to have a more objective view, may give you an easier opportunity to make a statement about the person's ability to act with tolerance.

How we as individuals relate to tolerance is of the greatest importance for our identity.

As I have made Compromise part of the heading and claim it as a condition for tolerance to be practised, I will dwell a little on this word.

One explanation goes as follows: "A Compromise is a result of actions where no one of the parties gets its will 100%, but everyone gets something".

Apart from Love, Compromise, may be one of the most important words.

Even when using the expression "unconditional love", there is a need for a little Compromise at time.

Reaching out your hand to your enemy is, I believe, not the same as turning the other cheek. In principle I am totally for the one with the cheek, but life experience has taught me that this approach seldom results in success. The reason being that man is his own worst enemy.

On the other hand, to reach out a hand as a start, particularly when it is done with good will, does not result in an either/or situation, meaning that you either get a slap when you turn the other cheek, or you do not.

Maybe I have reached this conclusion after having had dogs most of my life, before I became a pensioner.

From when I was only six, my best friend was our English Setter.

Having to do with dogs, you know that the best way to approach a strange dog, is to carefully stretch out your hand.

You will quickly experience if this invitation to closer contact is successful.

Luckily, I have still both hands with full sets of fingers and have only the best experience with this approach.

I will not dwell further with this comparison. Everyone has their own experience, but what I try to emphasize is that the situation is not black or white.

Unfortunately, we humans have a sad tendency to make things black or white. Everything becomes easier by making things black or white, but also thus more incorrect.

A Balanced Tolerance with the aid of Compromise is necessary. Give a little and take a little, none of the parties feel they are with their back against the wall.

To simplify everything is not always the best solution, understood as looking at the situation as black or white. Because of such simplifications, often unnecessary discontent occurs, resulting in Tolerance with the aid of Compromise being put to a big test.

Tolerance is an ingredient in a variety of situations, without me dwelling to much on it. The total lack of tolerance related to the acceptance of different religions, is probably what has caused the biggest challenges on our planet throughout time.

Maybe not so strange as this is where we find the most fanatics, clearly examples of people with black or white opinions.

***

MY FOOD FOR THOUGHT ON
TOLERANCE

TOLERANCE I
Tolerance stands for patience and the acceptance of other people's opinions.
Where the ceiling is high, the volume is always greater and there's more room to play with. Opposites attract it is said,
and there's probably a lot of truth in that, but not without tolerance.

From a wedding speech in 2005

TOLERANCE III
It costs, but you don't lose much of yourself by being Tolerant.

2018

TOLERANCE AND BALANCE
If you are Tolerant without being taken for granted, you can achieve a better Balance in yourself.

April 2019

TOLERANCE AND COMPROMISE I
Tolerance is a balancing act and Compromise is the weight on the scales that makes it balance.

2016

TRUTH

March 2014

When you hear the expression, "The truth is…", then be on the alert.

In my opinion, anyone using this phrase lacks an understanding of reality.

A person using the expression, "The truth is…" without immediately adding "in my opinion", is lacking any form of credibility.

What is true and isn't, is, unfortunately a stretchy concept for many.

The expression, "the Truth is…" is just as hopeless as described in an earlier reflection, which was called "Honesty".

It's easy to mix the use of the word's truth and honesty. In many ways, they go together, but of course do not.

I never heard anyone say, "This is my honest truth". If that was the case, the reason must have been to underline the truth.

Think about it. In this case, first you emphasize your "honesty", underlining you're general honest. Second you make the mistake of telling the "Truth" unconditionally. The truth for whom?

Typically, this case demands an amendment such as, for example, "Subjectively, this is my honest truth".

Anyhow, in my opinion, there is, nevertheless, a big difference between the words truth and honesty.

The truth, even when being treated sloppily by many, is of course not stretchy, it's black or white. Either it is true or it's not true, or it's false.

The closest example I can come up with to put this concept of "the incorrect truth and the correct truth" into a more understandable light, is to have a look at the media.

Probably today's most dominating media outlet for news and information, is the TV.

Of course, there is also the written press together with a lot of social media, which is increasingly used in conjunction with modern technology.

This however is much too comprehensive to deal with in a little reflection like this.

I stick to the TV and imagine that there are more than 30000 television stations in the world.

No use to touch the countries working with only state-controlled TV. In my opinion, in such cases the "correct truth" never reaches the population.

With tens of thousands of channels, it's obvious there are equally many influencing possibilities.

In Europe alone there are more than 11000 channels available. It's not as if they all transmit news, of course, or that they perform in any way a conscious influence on us viewers; but within all genera they focus on truth. Some of them like to be the carrier of truth, and others claim they are the one presenting the "correct truth".

I will limit myself to one example which I, in turn, think is quite engraving. There is no reason to hide which channel I'm referring to – I mean CNN; a news channel claiming to be the largest in the world.

Here I got to know by one of the top journalists, in an advertisement to promote the channel, that she had a new twist on her reporting, she was going to tell the truth. Important for us listeners to know.

As far as I remember, after continuous repetition, it

was taken off after a few months; so obviously someone must have discovered the blunder.

From my perspective, the essential thing when dealing with the truth, is that you see it in conjunction with objectivity.

The person or people claiming that their channel stands for the "correct truth" must, if they look for credibility, emphasize that they present their information based on their own objective review. It means that they have judged the truth of the information in question from the outside, put themselves in a position to objectively look at all sides of the case.

One thing is the objective attitude towards the truth, but do you have time to go into all the details, and is it really that important?

The news comes first they say; and of course it's important to be the first.

Correctness, meaning the truth. Yes, of course, it's important that what's presented is true, but at the same time it's even more important that the number of viewers are retained and increased?

This happens only if the public feel that the channel in question is delivering.

The fact that an enormous number of channels are available must not be forgotten. Many of them are transmitting content where the truth is not looked upon as being important. Could it be that all channels on TV have their own norms about the truth, and that they are based on the owner's assumptions, attitude, and economic interests?

What happens to the truth in the middle of all this? So-called "authentic reporting" must also be mentioned.

"Authentic" defines something as genuine, original or something having its own character. Nothing is mentioned about truth, and that's maybe not necessary?

Maybe it's easier for the TV companies to identify themselves with an authentic form of truth. Is that truth more tolerant than the general truth?

The expression: "The truth may be in between" may for many seem logical; but does anyone believe that if you take news from RT (Russian Television) and CNN and divide them in two, you get the correct truth?

Maybe an extreme example as I have understood that the RT channel is state controlled.

Could there be anything in the saying, "the origin of truth, the source, can be the truth's worst enemy"?

Unfortunately, nothing in the world can be ideal, so maybe we must accept the truth we are faced with in daily life and use our common sense.

***

MY FOOD FOR THOUGHT ON TRUTH

TRUTH AND UNTRUTH

What is despairing is that Truth for someone is Untruth to others.
The golden middle way cannot be used in terms of Truth and Un-
truth.

2018

TRUTH AND LIES I

Whoever possesses Truth is rich
- while the Liar for all time will remain poor.

TRUTH AND LIES II

If the claim that everyone is right based on their beliefs is correct,
and who can contradict that, there will be an infinite spectrum be-
tween the extremes of Truth and Lies.
The same will apply to information from so-called reliable sources.

2018

”THE TRUTH IS…”

Truths are correct for the person who uses the phrase: ”The truth
is…”, but will always reflect on his or her prerequisites.

December 2018

UNDERSTANDING

October 2013

Think what a difference it would make if we humans one day really understood one another. This is, of course, not black and white, as we mostly understand one another – at least with regard to major issues; but differences and disputes often occur because of our thinking that we have understood everything without this being the case; especially when it has to do with details, and small but important nuances.

There is usually no harm intended by either party, but often nuances causing misleading results.

Does this mean that in general we don't understand each other, and that there would be a marked difference in results on the day when we really do manage to understand one another? Yes, I believe so. We often don't understand one another, or don't take time enough to try to understand one another. This leads to unforeseen challenges in our narrow everyday lives, as well as in a larger national, inter- national, and global context.

First, we must recognise what is meant by fully understanding one another.

Here it isn't just that we speak different languages. Misunderstandings can be fertile ground for disagreements, even when both parties communicating, seemingly speak the same language.

In simple communication the main issues are usually understood. Nuances and details, however, often count for more than you can imagine.

This is what we must realize if any of the content in this reflection is to make sense.

You must realize that when you delve into a communication, nuances can easily be downplayed or disappear, and the deeper meaning often is not evident or understood.

Many of us can't see this, which is probably only to the good, as we don't all have to delve so deeply into details.

I have my own experience when it comes to different languages and understanding.

My wife is Swiss, and since she comes from Geneva her mother tongue is French.

I don't speak French and have for various reasons never had the inclination to learn this language, so our communication takes place in English. In both our cases, this was not the language used at the beginning of our lives; it was not our own and we both had to learn it.

She has lived in Spain for more than forty years and was married to an Englishman for more than twenty, whereas my English comes from school in Norway, living abroad in a predominantly English environment and from business.

Her vocabulary is extensive, whereas mine is more limited. Despite this, I find that our everyday communication functions very well.

We have also been part of the "vintage" category for some time now, and this undoubtedly has its advantages as regards communication, since maturity often means acquiring more tolerance, at least according to yourself.

It becomes easier to make allowances for misunderstandings, when communicating in a language which is foreign to both parties, and when you have a smidgen of tolerance.

Understanding is not always positive, however.

The so-called know-it-all, who supposedly understand it

all, aren't necessarily entirely likeable, but this doesn't mean, of course, that those who have no understanding whatsoever, automatically can be labelled as likeable.

Expressions like, "I understand your point of view", or such, are frequently used in diplomatic circles, where it often has to do with making approaches through give and take. When results are to be achieved through understanding and tact, details and nuances are important.

In political contexts, appeals are often made to show understanding, thus calling for diplomatic solutions.

Can we learn to understand one another better?

For me it's quite clear that we can, if we first acknowledge that it is often understanding the details and nuances, which make for a better relationship.

If you are conscious of this, you can in various contexts, through the seeking of common understanding, go a long way towards reaching more agreement.

***

MY FOOD FOR THOUGHT ON
UNDERSTANDING I

UNDERSTANDING I

Those who think that I don't have it, have evidently not Understood - that things have been let happen which I later saw should have been halted. For the very simple reason that development takes place through sacrifice and vision, not by putting a calculated stop to the mission. It has cost to sow - the profits maybe low - but it's worth the Understanding I have gathered up to now.

UNDERSTANDING II

A well-known expression is that the most dangerous are those who themselves do not Understand that they do not Understand. However it does not mean that you are blameless even if you admit that you don't Understand.

Nov. 2019

UNDERSTANDING III

For those who do not Understand, no problems exist.

July 2019

UNDERSTANDING AND DECISIONS

All Decisions, if they are meant to have any value, must be based on Understanding, thus on the will to Understand the matter and the parties involved.

March 2013

WILL

May 2014

Unlike physical strength, I see the human will as an unbelievably strong resource. A strong-willed person often gets that term just because she or he stands for having a strong will.

First, we must clear away the will related to stubbornness, the one occurring specially in kids and adolescents.

Not that this type of will necessarily disappears because of you have grown up; but for those that it applies to there will always be problems.

The will I have in mind is the positive will, the one that makes thoughts and meanings grow to new heights.

The will to understand is one of several good examples of a positive will. You may as well call it the ground-breaking will.

If you are to reach a goal you have set for yourself, whatever the type, the will must be there.

It's not the case at all that if only the will is there, you automatically reach all the goals you have set for yourself.

A will is only one of the ingredients needed to do so, but maybe the one that at the end of the day is the condition needed to put your thoughts and meanings forward.

Back to the positive will, the will to understand.

For me it's totally clear that no challenges can be overcome if you don't have the will to do so, and if you want to be able to overcome them, you must understand both the challenges and those involved.

Your will is a power which, when properly used, is incredibly strong.

People glowing with positive willpower normally have their understanding in order.

But and this is important, it must be a positive, natural will and not one which is forced.

The will can, in some people, be destructive and effacing if seen in conjunction with negativity – negative will.

In this context it is a matter of people with weak will- power, or people with no will. No positivity can come from having weak willpower or being without a will.

I have little experience of how these expressions are used in daily life, but I presume that they are quite similar when it comes to performance, although they are of different gravity.

If you have week willpower, the will still plays a role, although minor. If, on the contrary, you are without will, it means that you are devoid of will. In this case you are badly off for action.

Anyhow, all this is just a lot of theory, of course. How the will is perceived by each one of us in our daily life, remains something we should not dwell on too often.

There are plenty of other things our brain must cope with.

***

MY FOOD FOR THOUGHT ON
WILL

THE WILL TO UNDERSTAND
The Will to Understand as well as the desire and faith that you shall succeed, is a condition for reaching your goals.

THE WILL TO WIN
It is easy to remind yourself that the W in the Will is the first letter, in the same way that Winning starts with a W. That is exactly what it is all about. If you lack the Will to Win, it is like giving up. In this context it's about overcoming the challenges.

January 2019

WILL AND UNWILLINGNESS
The positive Will and the Will to understand are the most important Wills - while Unwillingness will always be negative.

WILL IS FUNDAMENTAL
The Will to understand is Fundamental. If the Will is failing because the understanding fails, the result is halting.

May 2014

Fairness is an important element in everyone's life - especially in early childhood and adolescence. That's because it is in this phase of your life that you become acquainted with fairness for the first time, often in connection with accusations of various kinds, both true and false.

As soon as your upbringing starts to focus on what's right and what's wrong, and that's one of the first things you are confronted with, you become acquainted with accusations.

Accusations are a completely natural occurrence in your upbringing.

If at an early stage in your development you have a clear concept of what is right and what is wrong, you are indeed lucky, but it can hurt a lot the first time you suffer a false or wrong accusation.

If you are accused of something you have done and know deep down that you have done it and that it was wrong, other factors are brought in automatically. You must consider whether you want to admit to it or not. If you believe that the consequences of making an admission will be major it's only human to deny the accusations, as you can frequently see.

Lies are probably one of the first things you learn about in life, as early on you must test how far you can toe the line and what consequences it has when you overstep it.

Perhaps a separate reflection about the lie would be a good idea, but that'll have to wait until a more suitable occasion.

The false accusation or the incorrect one is the one which really hurts. It can, of course, be based on a lack of information, which might easily have been obtained and thus it helps create even greater misunderstanding.

Case dismissed without further consequences, but if the incorrect accusation is so one-sided and steadfast that it can't be disproved, then things might become dangerous.

I was far from an exemplary pupil. Homework was almost non-existent and if I could make mischief, for which I had a great ability, I did. Naturally enough, seen from the point of view of the teachers, it thus became very easy to blame me, even for things I hadn't done. I can't recall any serious charges, but even the few times it happened, it was extremely painful.

The sense of fairness is for most of us a strong one.

If not, how can it be possible to commit such an injustice?

So-called "justice murder", which is what a miscarriage of justice is called in Norwegian, is probably at the top of the list when it comes to incorrect accusations. (According to Wikipedia the expression miscarriage of justice is used when a person has been convicted in a court of law of a crime he or she hasn't committed.)

Originally the Norwegian expression was used when someone was wrongly convicted and sentenced to death, but as this method of punishment became less common or was finally abolished, the expression has been given an extended meaning. The strong word "murder" illustrates the criminal act which contributes to or causes an innocent person to be sentenced and detained.

Fortunately, miscarriages of justice don't happen too often, but imagine what a meaningless and desperate situation a person must be in when it does happen. I would like to include the details of a recent personal experience.

My wife's newly acquired white-painted Hyundai i30 was

parked in its normal place, in front of our apartment, while we were away for a few weeks, as we had used my car to travel to the airport.

Back home again and almost immediately after we had brought our suitcases inside, the doorbell rang. The caretaker, who also keeps an eye on our apartment when we're away, informed us that, just a couple of days after we had left, he had seen a certain neighbour, back his blue-painted car, also a Hyundai but a larger model, out of the car park. By accident or poor judgement, he scraped along the side of my wife's car and left some heavy blue marks on the white paint. We had already noticed, when we parked after arriving home from the airport, that his car, which before we left had various small dents on the right side, had been newly painted and was without a scratch.

We knew that he had previously backed into one of the outside lights in the driveway and broken it, but how any new dents had been acquired was, of course, none of our business.

The following day my wife got in touch with the neighbour and in their mother tongue, which is French, she appraised him of the damage to her car.

To her consternation he denied that he had anything to do with it and pointed out that his newly painted car was without a scratch. I've seldom seen such nerve, but then he happens to be a very unpleasant person.

The neighbour in question rents the house he's living in, and I doubt that he'll ever read this, but should he happen to do so, I hope he'll understand why we now completely ignore him.

We could, of course, have taken him to court, and experienced a lot of frustration as a result, but life is too short for such things at our age.

This is one of those cases where you put up your hands and say to yourself:

"Where there is nothing, even the emperor's power ceases".

Here I don't have any material things in mind, poor man.

People of his kind probably think of themselves as winners; after all, he was spared the expense.

***

**MY FOOD FOR THOUGHT ON
ACCUSATIONS AND LIES**

ACCUSATION I

*If you are accused of something you have done and you are aware
that you have done it and that it was wrong, the assessment comes
as to whether it is something you want to admit or not.*
2014

ACCUSATIONS II

The false accusation is the one that really stings.
2014

ACCUSATIONS III

*Defending that "correct" accusations be rejected cannot be recom-
mended.*
2014

ACCUSATIONS IV

*If at an early stage in your development you have a clear concept of
what is right and what is wrong, you are lucky,
but it can sting extra hard when you first become acquainted with
a crazy or incorrect accusation.*

CONCENTRATION AND FOCUS
March 2013

Concentration is an ability which I need to improve. How can someone be capable of claiming such a thing? How can someone say for sure that they have the capability to concentrate or, as in my case, that I need to improve my ability to concentrate.

How can it be measured?

Concentration means to be so involved in something that everything else disappears.

Now I must concentrate on getting on with this reflection. In other words, I must focus on the task, get so involved in it, that everything else disappears. How do I do that? Is it like looking down into a funnel where you suddenly see everything quite clearly at the bottom; eureka?

Is there a connection between concentrating and focusing?

A lot of questions with answers few and far between.

If there's something you can't do at any given time, it's easy to blame your lack of concentration.

In the world of sports, the terms concentration and focus are well known.

Nobody wins if their concentration is absent, and they lose the ability to focus on the task at hand.

This is especially obvious in the types of sports which stretch over time, but where there is a constant need for precision performance.

As in many other contexts, golf comes to mind here.

In a space of about four hours, which is what a round of golf should take, you must perform as few strokes as possible. All of them can be different and there are up to 14 different clubs to choose from.

Around 70 strokes and below per round, applies only to the very best players, while just over a hundred is the more normal number.

Each stroke requires full concentration and focus and the least disturbance, whether it be from the players themselves or in the form of unwanted thoughts and movements.

Any external influences can have dramatic consequences.

Regardless of the type of sport, it's often the ability to concentrate and focus that determines the winner.

Here is a typical example of my own lack of the ability to ignore external disturbances in a sporting context.

Before I got into golf, I was an active clay pigeon shooter for many years, specifically in the area called skeet.

I'll never forget the episode in which, during a championship's competition over 100 clays, I had fought my way through 99 hits and was ready for clay number 100. There was no lack of spectators, but not a sound to be heard.

One more hit would lead to a new Norwegian record for 100 clays, so with my nerves totally on edge, I got ready for the last clay. Just as I called for the clay, which is thrown from a machine in a tower at an acoustic signal from my voice, I heard a voice say loud and clear: "Now he'll become Norwegian Champion".

The shot went off the moment I got a glimpse of the clay. That was it. The amazing thing was that the person making the statement was the reigning champion.

The result was thus equal to the old record which was, of course, a big disappointment for me. It's quite possible that I would have missed anyway, but, once again, at moments like this, the deciding factor is the ability to concentrate and focus.

Apart from Gold - Silver - and Bronze medals in Norwegian team Championships, my best achievement was a bronze medal in August 84 in the open Norwegian Championship.

Up until the last 25 clays, I was often well placed for top positions. The skill was obviously there, but the lack of my ability to concentrate, focus and control my competition nerves right to the end will have to take the blame.

My practise rounds were at times equal to the international top ones in those days. The best practice round ever was 197 out of 200.

For your information, in my days, normal skeet competitions lasted for two days, on which 100 clays were shot each day, so there were many waiting periods and distractions. Today, as far as I know, the rules have changed.

It's far easier for me to concentrate when it comes to finding solutions to technical challenges.

Then it's easier to suppress other disturbing factors.
But then you are immersed in yourself – not exposed like during a competitive sport.

It is said that you can train your ability to concentrate. This I don't doubt. What I question, however, whether it's just as easy to get your competition nerves under control.

It is quite clear that some people have better control over their nerves than others, and I also have no doubt that there are those who have a far better ability to concentrate and focus than others.

MY FOOD FOR THOUGHT ON
CONCENTRATION AND FOCUSING

FOCUSING

Whatever happens around you - Focus on what you stand for with humility but stick to your principles as otherwise you will lose focus.

July 2019

FOCUS AND VISION

Focusing on the goal is the most important of all - while Vision is needed to check that all conditions are in place to reach it.

CONCENTRATION AND FOCUSING I

When there is something you cannot achieve, it is easy to blame it on a lack of concentration and focus.

2013

CONCENTRATION AND FOCUSING II

There is no doubt that some people have better control over their nerves than others. Those who daily depend on being top equipped in this context will work on that matter, while the rest of us can use the time for other, for us, more important tasks.

2023

CONSEQUENCES
March 2014

The word consequence says very little. The word can be used in many contexts, one of them being to bear the consequences of your actions.

In my speech at the confirmation of my grandson, Nicolas, in September 2013, I touched on the theme consequences and that there are, for me, three stages of consequences, related to our actions, all of which count in the development of human beings.

I quote some excerpts from the speech given on the 7th of August 2013:

First there is unconscious consequence.
That's the one all children instinctively use in their development. How far can I toe the line before I overstep it, and before there are unpleasant consequences? You have throughout the years been a very frequent user of this method, Nicolas, and it seems at times, that you cross the line with the clear idea that it'll be exciting for you to see what will happen next.
This procedure is, as I've said, used by all children and is a healthy one, although it might at times be a trial for the parents.

The next one is conscious consequence.
All actions have consequences in one form or other. As time goes by you learn, however, what the consequences of your actions will be, though you often go ahead anyway. You obviously learn from it, even though it at times can result in a black eye or maybe worse. You also learn that consequences are not always the same each time even though there is the

same sort of action. So, this may result in new and surprising experiences. It takes time to learn from this, something which can also be costly.

If you don't act at all, you'd think you got away with it, but then you're lagging behind in terms of experience and that can easily delay the process. To find some middle way would be my advice in this case.

The third one is a governing consequence.
That's the one where, before acting, you carefully consider the consequences.

The action doesn't take place until you have a clear idea of its consequences.

When you have reached this stage, you decide whether the action is worth its consequences and is thus well equipped for your ongoing journey through life.

You easily become confused if you look more closely at what is really meant by the word consequence.

One encyclopaedia defines consequence as a logical follow up to a prior action. This can be a fact arrived at empirically or logically, or an event-related reason for it to happen. One action may easily have several consequences.

Take a closer look at this explanation of a consequence and see if it becomes clear to you; I am having a bit of a problem with it.

Enough said, Nicolas at least seemed to think that he had understood its meaning. I can't imagine that he paid attention to the empirical or logical aspects of it; the word consequence is just something you understand intuitively, even at an early age.

The word empirical comes from the Greek "empiri", which in turn means "experience related". Not that I think you didn't already know it, but I looked it up just in case. As for the logical part, there's no need for further comment.

As for Nicolas, I believe he has a strong "empirical" reason for his understanding of consequences.

One of the consequences of having a big mouth might be that you get hit on the head. No reason to conceal that this has happened to me a few times, but it was in my early adolescence, long before I had a clear idea about consequences.

The older you get, the more experience and the better equipped you are to analyse the consequences of your actions; but you will probably never manage to avoid all the bad ones. Neither do you necessarily wish to avoid all consequences, as there are also positive ones from time to time, which you want to experience.

Oh yes, there are good consequences lying in wait all the time, even though the word consequence is used most often in unhappy circumstances.

An example of a good consequence might be that you have done a favour for someone, which has been significant for the person concerned.

The consequence then is that you get a good feeling, which is often worth much more than any other type of reward.

If you think about it, there are many actions in your everyday life which can lead to good consequences, not least among people who are close to one another. A little attention, which often costs nothing, can result in incredibly good consequences. But be aware, an unintentional word at the wrong time can lead to unintentional consequences.

At the end of last year, my wife and I undertook an action which was to have significant consequences.

I grew up with dogs and always had, up until I married my present wife, at least one English setter. As a consequence of this, I believe in all modesty to possess a certain amount of experience when it comes to dogs. My wife had a short-haired dachshund for many years before we met each other, more than twenty years ago, so she also knows what it means to have a dog. Anyway, as a consequence of acquiring her last dog – fully grown –, after a divorce had prevented the previous owner from keeping it, it was both housebroken and well behaved, so she had no experience with puppies. And to make everything clear, I must also add that it had been more than twenty years since I had had my last English setter.

On my wife's initiative, after having talked it over for some time, weighing the pros and cons, we decided in late autumn last year to check into the possibility of acquiring a little short-haired dachshund. I should add that dog number two during my first marriage was a compromise. As it wasn't too easy to have a hunting dog in a flat, we decided on a rough-haired dachshund. I wasn't going to use it for hunting purposes, as I only shot birds during my hunting days.

Because of having ordered it, the day came when the owner of the local pet shop in Vera, our nearest town, informed us that our short-haired dachshund "Duke", as it was already called by the breeder, was on its way from Toledo.

Since at that point in time we happened to be in Portugal playing golf, he consequently offered to keep it at his place for the week it would take us to get back.

All was well, and the day of the big event came, when we went to pick up our new, four-month-old family member.

The pet shop owner already had a French bulldog about four years old and, when we met the two at the shop, it was clear that little Duke had already gained some respect. The owner told us that, from the very first day, the little puppy had made it clear who got to eat first. The consequence of Duke's behaviour was that the French bulldog had immediately accepted the situation.

At the same time as we picked up Duke, my wife bought a lot of necessary equipment, such as a transport crate for travels complete with blanket, a bed to be placed in our little office, where we had decided the dog would sleep, a collar, a dog leash, fastening devices for car transport and some nappy-like rugs for the liquid and more solid stuff, which forms a natural part of everyday life. Furthermore, there was food, treats and some toys for encouragement, with and without a built-in squeaky noise. The excitement was great, and Duke passed water from pure pleasure every time we tried to pick him up.

The car had been equipped with a colourful plaid blanket, which we'd bought in Scotland earlier in the year, and which we thought would be good for him to get used to in the car.

Back home in the flat Duke immediately settled in.

Another Scottish blanket was put on one of the sofas, the one my wife normally uses, as we thought that's where the dog should stay when all three of us were at home and he felt the need to rest.

A couple of the nappy-like blankets were placed on the floor, while our new family member inspected each centimetre of the office, passageway, and the open kitchen section of the sitting room as well as the sitting room itself.

Because of his short legs, he couldn't get onto the sofa on his own, so each time he tried to do this, he was lifted. No sooner was he up there, however, before he jumped down again and disappeared into the office, immediately returning with one of his toys in his mouth. And so it went, non-stop, until he was completely exhausted. Finally, he was sleeping like a baby until a short time later he was going full speed again.

On his travels he was sometimes out of our sight and as a consequence of our not being able to see him, he took the opportunity to do his business.

The rugs meant for this purpose were, of course, bone dry.

To make a long story short, all that was left to do was to put him in his bed in the office, turn out the light and shut the door.

As it was clear that Duke was my wife's dog, as we all know there can only be one boss, she was the one to carry out the procedure. The big question, of course, was how he would react to it.

To our great surprise, no sound was heard from him until well after seven the next morning. Then, however, there was a lot of activity going on in the office.

We heard whining and tiny whimpers, and claws scratching the door. It turned out that it was not the door to the passage and freedom that was being attacked, but the cupboard door hiding the dry dog food.

We had closely followed the instructions for meting out meals, but already after just a few days of him showing constant hunger, the consequence was a slight upward adjustment of the food quantities.

The same ritual took place each morning. My wife in slippers and housecoat, collar, and plastic bag at the ready, following behind a tail-wagging Duke, hoping that he would do his business outside. Unfortunately, a hope was usually all it was, in which case it didn't take many minutes from the time they got back in until he proudly showed us how clever he was, but seldom on the intended rugs.

We had at first decided to keep the door leading to our bathroom and bedroom shut. Everything inside there was to be out of bounds for Duke. After a bit of back and forth, using both index finger and a stern voice, it was also OK to leave the door open, so long as he could see one of us inside; but as soon as we went from the passageway into the bathroom or bedroom, it naturally became too much. Seconds later he was on his way in. The consequence being that the door remained closed most of the time. There are limits to what one can expect from a puppy, after all.

The greatest consequence of all in this case came after four weeks of having the most beautiful little puppy in the world. Practical experience and common sense told us that we were simply too "mature" to deal with the consequences resulting from having to raise a new family member and changing the lifestyle we had become used to after fifteen years.

My wife brought the matter up with the owner of the pet shop one day when she was passing by. He told her that both his wife and daughter had been very sad when they had had to give Duke away after the week he'd been there, but for obvious reason they had said nothing about it to us.

He said they had already become very fond of him.

As a consequence of this, my wife asked him if he would consider taking over the responsibility for Duke. He straight away consulted his family, who immediately and with great enthusiasm looked forward to the new addition to their family.

When I say that everyone was looking forward to it, I can't vouch for the French member of the family but have since been told that they live together beautifully.

The somewhat sad consequence for us now is the loss of Duke after the four weeks we had together.

The positive consequence is that we can visit him whenever we like, and we experience the joy of seeing that he not only has a good home but also another dog as a friend – even if it is a Frenchman who has quite clearly learnt to live with the consequences of having acquired a little brother.

Did you notice the great number of times I used the word consequences in this story? How many do you think there are? You guessed right, the word is mentioned fifty-two times.

So, as you can see, there is hardly a thing which, in some form or other, doesn't have consequences. I could easily have troubled the reader with more, but then this reflection would probably have had even more unintended consequences.

***

MY FOOD FOR THOUGHT ON
CONSEQUENCES

CONSEQUENCES I

*Examples of three stages of Consequences, all of which count in the
development of human beings:*
*The unconscious consequences - The conscious consequences and the
governing consequences.*

CONSEQUENCES II

*The Consequences of giving someone the little finger can be fateful
if you don't know them.*
Nov. 2019

CONSEQUENCES - INCONSISTENCIES

*Everything you do can have big or small Consequences.
Inconsistencies or lack of Consequences are achieved when you are
inactive.*

CONSEQUENCES - DEVELOPMENT

*That children toe the line as far as they can before they experience
Consequences is part of their Development.
How is it that the adults constantly continue to ignore them?
Do they never learn?*
Sept. 2019

CURIOSITY

March 2013

"I wonder what I will get to see, beyond the lofty mountains". I'm not quite certain who wrote this, but I believe that it was the famous Norwegian writer Bjørnstjerne Bjørnson.

In my opinion it symbolizes curiosity. "The eye will surely meet nothing but snow".

Supposition, nothing certain, what else, curiosity.

Was it a quote from Bjørnson or someone else? Am I not curious about that?

Not really, I probably don't have the capacity to be curious about everything; that would be too time-consuming. There must be priorities.

For the sake of this reflection, I had to check it anyway and, sure enough, it was Bjørnson. "Around and about there are nothing but trees, I would very much like to get across; when will I ever dare?"

You would think after this that everyone has certain subjects for their curiosity.

If there is some truth in any of this, we're all curious, but for most of us our curiosity is limited to that which we feel strongly about or are especially interested in. In other words, the interesting question is not whether we are curious or not, as everyone is curious to some extent or other.

Does this mean that if you don't have the ability to ask questions, or are indifferent to finding answers to your questions, or if you haven't got any questions at all, then you are lacking in curiosity?

Probably yes; but again, most people find ways of showing their curiosity within their areas of interest, and thus find answers to their questions.

There's nothing wrong in that, as we don't all have to be the same. In my case, curiosity is the same as being and feeling alive.

I see it as a driving force, that which makes you put one foot in front of the other in your everyday life.

Curiosity is the driving force behind progress.

Forget the curiosity which makes you poke your nose into other people's business, as that seldom leads to anything good, and you're better off without such information.

It's the curiosity which asks questions beginning with "why?" which, in my mind, is the important one.

Again, when you don't ask questions, you remain single-minded, you come to a halt and don't get any further. It's good that I've concluded that we all have degrees of curiosity.

In November 1994 I wrote the reflection "Why?".

When I refer to events during my time at school in Italy as a 17–18-year-old, I wasn't as aware of things as I became later in life. That's why I asked questions like: "What makes us ask the question "Why?" so often. Is it because we're curious or because we're ignorant?"

Back then, I saw "why?" from a completely different angle to the one I saw it from later, but perhaps it helped me become aware of the word as I understand it today.

My angle then had more to do with language and communication, than with the more general significance of curiosity as the driving force behind progress.

Can you be curious about curiosity, or is that gilding the lily? Do you in that case end up in a never-ending circle? If you're curious about something, without having found the answer, you can, of course, assume an answer and renew your curiosity on that basis.

I've always been into technical challenges and have in all modesty found solutions to various of such challenges. As you can see, I prefer to call them challenges instead of problems, and these solutions have led to both patents and the manufacture of new products.

The expression "problems" is negative, whereas the word "challenges" trigger solutions.

This sidestepping is another matter altogether, but I'm convinced that everyone who has had anything to do with product development will agree, that to find satisfaction in this field you must be curious and look at "why?" from the above-mentioned angle.

Curiosity is the driving force behind progress.

I'm curious as to whether anyone has got anything sensible out of this, but I'm not really interested enough to ask. It could result in my having a set-back, which would reduce my curiosity and, as you may have understood, I would rather not lose it.

***

MY FOOD FOR THOUGHT ON
CURIOSITY

CURIOSITY
Curiosity is the driving force behind progress.
2013

CURIOSITY ABOUT LIFE
You can well be Curious about Life and at the same time have
a nature that is nailed to the earth.
2017

CURIOUS AND INDIFFERENT
Curiosity is the door opener for any development -
while Indifference gives rise to stagnation.

IN MY HEAD
In my Head there's a diode with thread -
and behind my look so quick, there's many a click.
To adjust, open and shut - the free circulation must never be cut.

DETAILS

2017

In many ways it's a pity that details matter, as they are mostly boring and time-consuming to get in place. I once wrote this about details in 2015.

"Many details are boring; but not all. For me, it's like details are often boring; but if it's about a detail needed to solve a challenge, I can be completely concerned about finding that detail, big or small."

Nevertheless, generally I am convinced that details matter, and that they are often boring.

I have dealt with "The Bagatelle". That reflection was written in April 1994 and starts as follows: "I'm a tiny bagatelle, a word, a smell, a taste. Spoken, felt or sensed, I can be a deciding factor in many contexts and of the greatest importance".

In the same way I believe it's often detailing that matter, and that is crucial.

It's often said that it's the small things that matter, here I am again, the bagatelle.

Doesn't it feel like a bagatelle is something small - a big bagatelle doesn't sound right, does it?

One of various definitions of a bagatelle is: "A small and less important case".

On the contrary, as I see it, a detail can be both small and big.

Anyway, maybe the detail is most often seen in conjunction with something small: "The only thing missing is the little detail".

To me this is more a matter of platitudes.

One of various definitions of a detail is: "Simplicity, part of a whole".

Well, "simplicity" has nothing to do with size and neither has "a part of a whole".

According to this, a detail gets more dimension, doesn't it?

A detailed report is by no means a bagatelle, just as details in an account are not.

Detailed descriptions of any kind one can only characterise as the opposite of having anything to do with a bagatelle.

If you look at examples like these, the "detail" and "the bagatelle" should not be used interchangeably.

Why on earth did I dig into these details, when I can clearly see the dimensions they can occupy?

I was taught about details in a non-academic way.

During my time training with Olivetti in northern Italy as a 17-18-year-old, I was taught to be a technical instructor. After my education, I was to teach our technicians, or mechanics as they were called in those days. At the end of the fifties everything technical was still mechanical.

Without going into too much detail, what is the difference between a technician and a mechanic?

According to Wikipedia, a technician is the professional title of a person with technical working tasks; while a mechanic is a craftsman using tools to repair machines.

As, among other things, a general agent for Olivetti office machines, our company Max Manus Kontormaskiner in Norway with its branches employed about 40 mechanics at the time and had a dealer network with many more.

In those days, a spade was called a spade.

No form of discrimination, but today I have the impression that all in this group are engineers, regardless of education, so in this context the details are probably not so important.

When it came to repairing Olivetti Divisumma 24 calculators with thousands of mechanical parts and more than a hundred adjustments of less than a millimetre, the details were of utmost importance.

Just one little wrong adjustment could be enough for the machine to fail after a repair, which means that that little detail could lead to the whole job being done over again.

Before I wrote this reflection, I googled "Olivetti calculators", hoping to find the exact number of parts the Divisumma 24 calculator consisted of, but I didn't find it.

As mentioned, many times in writing, I am hopeless when it comes to data. I'm not part of any social media and, as you can understand, I'm barely capable of navigating on google.

What strikes me, however, is that when I hit "enter" after having googled "Olivetti calculators", the first thing I see is a presentation of my book "70 years in communication" – about the Max Manus Companies from 1946 to 2016. (Norwegian edition, as it has not been published in English).

Of course, I understand that the Danish editor BoD (Bod. dk) are doing their marketing, but that googling "Olivetti calculators" should lead to my book is, in my opinion, quite clever.

I never got hold of the exact number of parts in the Divisumma 24, but that detail – even if it is a matter of a few thousand – is presumably not important for those who have cared to read this reflection about details.

***

MY FOOD FOR THOUGHT ON
DETAILS

DETAILS
In many ways, it's a pity that what matters are the Details, as they are often boring and time consuming to put into place.

DETAILS AND WHOLENESS
Too many Details are boring - while Wholeness is simpler.

DETAILS I
Detailed knowledge is not always necessary to make good decisions.
July 2023

DETAILS II
You can be knowledgeable without detailed knowledge.
July 2023

FANATICISM

May 2014

Even though it's probably clear to most of us what fanaticism means, I'll start, just in case, with a description from Wikipedia, which says that fanaticism is: "Extreme one-track mindedness. Enthusiastic claiming of personal convictions, often combined with wanting to persecute those who think or feel differently".

It almost makes me shudder when the word fanaticism is read or heard, or even just by thinking about it. Only in very special cases can I find something positive in connection with fanaticism, and then it has to do with personal fanaticism, for instance, when you are fanatically concerned about something special. In most cases, that kind of fanaticism is probably completely harmless.

Its limits are clear for most of us, but not for everyone, and that is probably what makes fanaticism so dangerous.

What I find somewhat strange is that one English description of fanaticism is in line with the above, in other words with the personal and harmless one. It goes like this: "Fanaticism is a belief or attitude involving uncritical eagerness or exaggerated enthusiasm as regards past-time activities or hobbies". Well, if that had been the only angle of fanaticism, lots of things would be different.

Many have tried throughout time to analyse the fanatic, he or she who stands for fanaticism. When that happens, it has mainly to do with that which most of us consider dangerous fanaticism.

The consensus seems to be that fanatics as such aren't evil in the strict sense of the word: they, the fanatics, are just fanatically convinced that the opinions they represent are the only correct ones. There is never any talk of compromise, seen from a fanatic's point of view, so the idea of using diplomacy where the fanatic is concerned, can be shelved at once. The greatest danger lies in the fanatic's ability to influence the weak or misguided, examples of which we see every day.

Well, of course, I'm not competent to add anything at all as regards fanaticism, but, on the other hand, I am concerned about having to put an end to this evil, the dangerous one, that is, once and for all. We must be realistic though, to believe that we can get rid of the dangerous fanaticism, is to aim too high.

If you want to try to do that, you must apply other measures, at least if you have a long-term solution in mind. Just imagine finding a sensible answer to that challenge.

In many areas it is totally acceptable to refer to statistics.

Of course, you can't always trust the statistics, but that has nothing to do with those involved not being able to gather the right material, but with the fact that the material has been manipulated for the statistics to show the desired result.

Regardless, there must be a statistic showing the percentage of the population who are fanatical according to the definition. I don't doubt that at all, but I believe there is a reluctance to making it official. It could lead to social consequences.

Is the percentage of people who are fanatical according to the definition – the dangerous one if it can be isolated –, greater, or smaller than five percent; or is it more than ten percent?

Is the percentage of the population who are fanatical according to the definition described in the English interpretation, greater or smaller than five percent, or is it more than ten percent? Would our knowing the size of the percentage have any significance at all for the rest of us in our daily lives?

Personally, I believe there are far more fanatics amongst us than we believe. In fact, I'd go so far as putting myself down as a potential candidate, as regards to the English interpretation, the one I believe to be harmless.

How can I say that? Well, there are things in our everyday lives that I can be fanatically concerned about, without my wanting to tell what they are.

This is because it has nothing to do with a permanent condition, and because I know that this form of fanaticism is a completely harmless one, at least for others. Whether it might be dangerous for me is another matter.

What I'm trying to say, in other words, is that fanaticism as such isn't necessarily dangerous. It's only if it's used incorrectly, according to most of us, that it becomes dangerous.

The dangerous fanatic is usually someone who chooses his followers with great care. Trust is created and solid friendships are made. The followers are usually simple and easily influenced people, and thus fit easily into the role of performing the evil transmitted through the relationship. In this role the fanatic is mortally dangerous.

If we stay with this latter description, of the dangerous fanatic, I trust that an honest statistic would verify that only a fraction of one percent of the population belongs to this category, at least in our part of the world, which is a good thing, if my assumption is correct.

Even if there is little each one of us can do to expose these potential "bomb threats", it is important that we make our beliefs and attitudes clear, so that we and those of like minds won't be subjected to unexpected ambushes.

MY FOOD FOR THOUGHT ON FANATICISM

FANATICISM AND OPINIONS

There is certainly a great deal of agreement that Fanatics as such are not evil, in the true meaning of the word. Fanatics are just Fanatically convinced that the Opinions they have are the only correct ones.

May 2014

THE FANATIC'S ENFORCER

The dangerous Fanatic is a good listener who carefully choose his Enforcer. Trust is created and solid ties are made. Enforcers usually consists of simple and easy-to-influence people, who thus act perfectly in the role as practitioners of the evil transmitted through the relationship with the Fanatic.

May 2014

FANATICISM I

There is never any question of compromise from the Fanatic's point of view, so, the idea of using diplomacy to resolve a conflict involving the Fanatic can be shelved immediately.

2014

FANATICISM II

There is probably little that each of us can do to expose these possible "bomb threats", but it is important that we have our attitude clear, so that we and our like-minded people do not become the subject of unexpected ambushes.

2014

FEELING OF GUILT

A feeling of guilt; it makes me shudder just thinking of it. Not that I believe I have reason to feel guilty, but there's no doubt that I'm one of those people who gives off an aura of guilt. This being the case even though I, at least in my own opinion, have no reason to do so.

Perhaps it has something to do with my adolescence.

I used to toe the line in my youth. There were seldom serious wrongdoings, but there was something about having to try things out. It's important to find out where to draw the line, as parents don't always offer appropriate guidelines.

If you are born with imagination and empathy, consequences are bound to follow.

My stepfather had a clear idea of where the line had to be drawn, everything he saw as a serious wrongdoing was measured in a certain number of strokes from the dog whip: it was as simple as that.

In many situations this is probably a good method of settling things, but according to today's standards apparently far from the right one. We mustn't forget that this was more than sixty years ago, and a lot was different in those days.

Enough said, I believe that I found the punishment just at the time. If I had crossed the line, that was the price I had to pay. Otherwise, the only alternative I could see to avoid the punishment was to run away from home. I don't believe that would have solved anything. I also don't believe my mother was quite in tune with the punishments but having a domineering husband, she chose to keep peace on the home front. At least I never registered any arguments between them on this subject.

The threat of being sent to the correctional institution on Bastøy in the Oslo fjord also remained in the background but was from my side probably never seen as a real possibility. In my opinion, that would be like shooting sparrows with a cannon. Nor did it ever happen.

We probably all experience a feeling of guilt in some form or other. You only have to look around among your family and friends. Whether the feeling of guilt is justified, only the person involved can say.

When I mentioned earlier on that those feelings of guilt may have to do with my adolescence, I was perhaps quite wrong. My younger half-sister, who never did anything wrong when she was little, has undoubtedly all her adult life had problems with her feelings of guilt. Could it have something to do with one's genes and not with one's upbringing?

In my case, the conscious feeling of guilt first occurred at school. There's no reason to hide that I was a so-called trouble-maker in class, but it was, as far as I remember, never suggested that whatever I did had a nasty intent.

It's strange to see, but my youngest grandchild, who is fifteen this year, has apparently had the same sort of struggle at school for the last few years. I have been given to understand that he is undoubtedly also a mischief-maker in class.

I have no difficulty facing reality today, and I see that many of the reprimands were justified.

But what about the other side of the coin? Often because of the above, you automatically got accused of things you hadn't done or taken part in? That was sometimes hard to swallow. It was thus registered as deeply unfair and difficult to understand.

So, I ask myself the question: is there a clear link between in- justice and feelings of guilt? I can't quite come to grips with it, but I have a feeling I'm on to something essential here.

This probably won't stop me using injustice as a separate theme for a reflection. It is, after all, a huge subject to write about when you think about all the injustice there is in the world.

Regardless, my feeling of guilt has fortunately decreased over the years.

At one time, I could never go through passport control without being called aside for a closer check.

The customs officers had a special eye for me, almost as if I was some sort of regular problem to them. I can't remember ever having been caught carrying anything I shouldn't have, or my "quota" having been exceeded. I don't want anyone to consider me sanctimonious in this context, but just because I believe my bad conscience could be sensed from afar, it was a contributing factor to my never carrying anything more than that which was within the allowable limits. This applies to the present as well as the past.

I mentioned the possible link between injustice and feelings of guilt, but now conscience comes into play.

I've already written a reflection about conscience. In it there is something about suppressing your feelings of a bad con- science and the warm glow you get from a good one. Con- science probably belongs in this reflection too, because I don't suppose there's anything called good or bad feelings of guilt, is there?

After this, the question will have to be changed to: is there a link between injustice, conscience and feelings of guilt?

It is time to get off this track before I start spinning out of control, as so far it has become complicated enough.

As some of you will have noticed, apart from my half-sister, it has so far only been about my own relationship to feelings of guilt. The reason for this must be that it is virtually impossible to describe other people's feeling of guilt, as that's a very private matter.

****

MY FOOD FOR THOUGHT ON
FEELINGS OF GUILT

FEELINGS OF GUILT I
We all have Feelings of Guilt in one form or another. If this feeling is justified or not, only the person with the Guilt can comment on.
May 2019

FEELING OF GUILT II
No one can describe the Feeling of Guilt of others.
May 2019

GUILT AND INNOCENCE
The feeling of Guilt is hard to bear - while the weight of Innocence is light as a feather.

FAULT
What would the world look like if we had no one to blame?
Oct. 2019

IGNORANCE

Why on earth am I dwelling on this word. Fortunately, it isn't used all that much, but when it is, it's usually in a serious context. If it is so that, in our daily life, we connect ignorance with stupidity, as I believe we tend to do, then that's wrong, in which case it might be worthwhile immersing ourselves a bit in ignorance.

I don't in any way wish to compete with Wikipedia or others who, in page after page, present all sorts of interpretations of the word. Perhaps I see something contradictory in the interpretations I'm dwelling on.

If ignorance has something to do with ignore, which sounds reasonable, it might seem a bit affected to say that to ignore means something like: "to refuse to take into account", whereas ignorance is described among other things as: "to pretend not to be aware of or know anything about this or that, or to be indifferent to".

If you look at the word ignorant, which must also have something to do with ignorance, then it is described, among other things, as: "to lack information about or knowledge of this and that". And in this context also: "to lack education or to be unsophisticated".

The word ignorant is further described as: "a person who is in a state of not being in the know; often used as an insult to describe those who ignore or discount important information or facts on purpose". I see this as being the same as: "to express yourself against better judgement".

It already becomes difficult for the average person to keep up, and these are only a few simple approaches.

I would probably not have started grappling with ignorance if I hadn't had a few experiences of my own related to the word. These I won't refer to, neither with names or situations, but more with attitudes, which I'm sure several people can identify with, either by doing a self-analysis or by examining their own experiences.

The ostrich is reputed to put its head in the sand when it senses danger. It then is supposed to believe itself to be invisible and thus can't be noticed. The ostrich is claimed to believe it is less visible and therefore feels safer, so what then has the ostrich got to do with my experiences of ignorance?

Well, even well-educated people, who are in no way stupid, can in certain situations act with ignorance.

Complete information can be available in all aspects of a case. It is also known with reasonable certainty that the people concerned do have all the information.

External indoctrination probably also plays an important role when it comes to behaviour patterns.

It happens again and again, however, that behaviour pattern shows that actual, available information is completely set aside, in other words, ignored, a fact which invariably displays ignorance on the part of those concerned. Or does it?

Is this then deliberate, or does it just happen? Is it a form of possible protection, like the ostrich act, or is it a fully conscious act? Again, we must make clear that: "Ignorance differs from stupidity, though both can lead to unwise actions".

As far as my own experiences goes, I choose to believe that some actions weren't fully conscious. Because when I choose to believe that the actions were deliberate, the whole thing takes on a more serious aspect, which might lead to much more serious consequences.

Good thing I'm tolerant.

Their actions are fully conscious. They know that they are talking against their better judgement, as that is what is necessary at times; it is this which, in my opinion, is unfortunate. Can it be described as a form of dishonesty?

If I stick to the earlier description of the word ignorant: "a person who is in a state of not being in the know; often used as an insult to describe those who ignore or discount important information or facts", then it's the one I adhere to when it comes to my own experiences.

Knowing full well that I may have misunderstood some details in my interpretation of ignorance, I'm right, at least according to my own assumptions. If you're curious as to what I mean by that, you can look at one of my earlier reflections: "What is right and what is wrong?".

I must admit, however, that even though I wasn't conscious of it, I may, in a pinch, have used this form of ignorance myself.

It wouldn't surprise me if to "express yourself against your better judgement" is considerably more widespread than I've assumed.

***

MY FOOD FOR THOUGHT ON
IGNORANCE

IGNORANCE I

A description of the word is: "To pretend that you don't know about this or that, or to be indifferent." Otherwise, intelligent people, in special contexts, can act with ignorance. Fully accessible information is present when it comes to all sides of a case, and it is known with reasonable certainty that those concerned are in possession of this information. Still, they speak out "against their better judgment".

October 2013

IGNORANCE II

If Ignorance has something to do with ignoring, it might seem a bit far-fetched that ignoring supposedly also means: "To refuse to pay attention to".

October 2013

THE OSTRICH GAME

The ostrich is known to bury its head in the sand when it is in danger. It thereby believes that it is invisible and is not noticed. The fact is that it is, of course, just as visible, while the self-deception makes it safe. If people who speak out against their better judgment are aware of what they are doing, the result can have serious consequences.

October 2013

IGNORANCE AND STUPIDITY

Ignorance differs from Stupidity, although both can lead to unwise actions.

October 2013

LIFE
2016

Life - who can describe life?

Life has different values in various cultures, and in some it seems like it has no value at all.

Fortunately, we know very little about life, apart from that it starts and at an unpredictable time ends.

In addition, another thing we know about it is that all of us are living it in one or another way, as long as we live. Most probably we live it as individually different as there are people on this earth, or, put in another way, as there are different fingerprints.

Some have big ambitions in life while others don't seem conscious of that property at all.

We are all different, arriving from different environments and belonging to different religions.

We live under different climates, belong to different forms of societies, and perform different tasks in the society we belong to.

Some claim that they are eligible to a larger portion of social benefits than others, and claim they deserve it, while others deal with the situation as it is and are happy that way.

Some need showing strength to keep their self-esteem, while others fully obey rules and regulations drawn up for what's right and wrong.

Others again, act as if they were the ones making the rules and regulations.

We all want to live, or at least most of us.

But when life is on its way to come to an end for whatever reason, and you are still conscious and clear, do you miss something? Specially if it happens at a young age.

You may at that stage not yet have got the big overview.

Do you ever in life get the big overview, and what might that consist of?

Even if you believe that you have found the answer to the big overview, will there still be something you miss, something you feel has not been done?

This theme is undoubtedly so personal, and its meanings so many, that it leads nowhere to go further.

Apart from that, you should not dwell too much on it either; time comes soon enough when too many of these thoughts come to mind.

When that happens it's presumably good, at least for some, to think about the life you have led, and how you have made use of it. Because that is life itself.

Is it likely that you ever get the big overview, and will you ever know what you missed?

"What is life, a breath in the sea, which descends......" by Adam Oehlenschlæger, is one most of us have heard about.

Søren Kirkegaard has a wonderful description of life:

"The day you came to the world, you cried while your close ones were happy. Live life so that the day you die, your close ones will cry while you're happy".

Imagine how simple things would be if we stopped worrying.

Samuel Johnson is in his full right stating:

"It's useless to worry about life; you won't get out of it alive anyhow"

I don't know who was the first one with this, but for me it has, for a long time, been a good rule of life that:

"Problems do not exist, only challenges".

"Live life as if you are going to die tomorrow" is a saying.

To me this sounds rather dramatic.

Should you fully follow this rule, you could be personally guilty in your short stay on mother earth.

If it is correct that most of us agree that life is an art of balance, something at least I advocate for, then maybe my own formulation in various ways illustrates this.

"Life is like a continuous surf. You must keep your balance until you reach land. Only then is it over".

After having written the above, it strikes me that so far, I have only mentioned life in conjunction with us people - extremely egocentric.

Our lives would of course not have existed if we were the only living creatures on earth.

After all, we are only one form of life among millions.

I'm not thinking about a life comparable with ours, but all forms of life needed to keep us humans going.

This is probably too much to comprehend.

We must only accept that, in one or another form, we are created, that we are a tiny little part of a whole, and that all life is dependent on one another.

The following "slogans" used these days in some TV channels, are a reminder in this context.

"If nature is not kept healthy, humans won't survive"; and the other from the nature: "If you don't take care of me, I can't take care of you".

Unfortunately, we humans are putting too much of a load on nature. Admittedly, at times we pull ourselves together and try to clean up misery, but only when we realise that we have let it go too far. That however is not good enough.

Maybe it's time we extend our thoughts about life from being egocentric "us selves first", to seriously consider how we – having the ability to act, after all can do something to keep a continuous balance in nature.

In this context, it must be added that a big group of us devote ourselves to improving our relationship to nature, which is good if it doesn't become fanatic.

We must never forget that if war breaks out between nature and ourselves, we will, no doubt, be the losers. There are plenty of challenges.

In my 78th year (2016) I reached the view that our cycle as individuals on this earth is magnificently adapted to our development.

Through our life we are constantly developing.

If we live long enough, we will see next generations starting where we left off, knowing that they will go through the same development as we did.

I don't believe those advocating that we can learn from experience gained by others. In life we must all gain experience ourselves, at times in a heavy way, not from others.

***

MY FOOD FOR THOUGHT ON
LIFE

LIFE I
*The best thing about Life is that it's yours. The most difficult can be
to acknowledge it, take the initiative and do something about it.*
To my daughter Anne-Marie on her 20th birthday

LIFE II
*The only thing we know about Life is that it's lived by all of us, in
one form or other, as long as we Live.*
2016

LIFE III
If you mean Life is different than you think, you are wrong.
Aug. 2019

LIFE UNTIL NOW
Until now I've lived Life - and experienced Life.
1995

OPINIONS

April 2014

If you haven't got an opinion about anything at all, you are, in my opinion, seemingly lost. Most of us, however, have opinions about most things, but having opinions isn't worth much if you don't know how to express them.

To have opinions and to be able to express them if you so wish is, at least in those democracies I'm familiar with, a privilege worth fighting for.

It is a human right which should never be taken for granted. We have all seen tragic examples of suppressed freedom of expression.

No debate on my part about freedom of expression; it ought to be taken for granted in an enlightened world, but the way I see it, that's not unfortunately the case everywhere.

Even though there is freedom of expression, it isn't necessarily so that when you have an opinion about something, you must express it, put things bluntly or fight on the barricades for it.

Furthermore, to keep certain opinions to oneself is a piece of advice I would like to give to all those who tend to spill over with them.

I don't believe that so-called normal people exist who don't have opinions about anything at all; everyone probably has opinions, it's part of the pulse of life.

On the other hand, those who have so-called convictions are perhaps few and far between. Anyway, as I've said, you don't need to fight for all your opinions, but when you have so-called hobby horses, understood to mean things you feel strongly about, then it's good to have convictions. It means that you stand by your opinions and fight for them.

Here you must, as in so many other contexts, be aware of the challenges connected to what many of us see as fanatical opinions and attitudes; but that's a totally different matter.

Fanaticism we'll put to one side in this case. It is scary enough as we've seen many examples of. Fanaticism is unfortunately everywhere, in all social, political, and religious fractions, and exists in almost all contexts. There is no doubt that we, for ever or at least for as long as human beings rule our world, will become acquainted with this unpleasant evil, fanaticism.

In early adolescence it is normally so that many of us are concerned with choosing what is right, according to the opinion of others, for fear of being looked upon as outsiders. Human beings are, as far as I know, defined as "pack animals", in this case to be understood as having identical beliefs: it makes us feel secure.

As you gradually start to feel comfortable with your life and more secure in yourself, you will form your own opinions about certain things, which will differ from those of others.

This I believe is related to the interests you have or acquire, but it is probably also a result of social and cultural influences. In many ways this is all well and good, as it is the fact that we aren't all the same, which adds spice to our respective lives.

We have something to compare with when, or better put if we can see our own opinions in relation to existing general norms. Many great personalities throughout time have had firm opinions about almost everything, which I believe is both reasonable and correct. Even though their opinions didn't always turn out to be the right ones, that's how it must be.

In order not to make the case too close to our time, we can use an example which goes back almost two thousand years in time. The then Roman Senator, Cato the Elder, is said to have ended all his speeches in the Senate with the subsequently famous sentence, here translated into English: "Furthermore I believe Carthage must be destroyed".

The reason for this was allegedly that he believed the city's wealth to be a threat to Rome.

Well, we can only hope that Cato the Younger, that is if he existed, learnt from this.

I have fought without success against firm collective opinions, virtually bordering on the fanatic. Whatever touch of diplomatic attitude I might have, immediately came up short, but it became a very special experience.

The time is the late eighties, and the place is Cabrera, the urbanization in the south of Spain where I had just begun my long-term plan to establish myself, when my retirement age was invariably reached – if I managed to live that long, that was.

I had already made good contact with the establisher and developer of the place, a very charismatic English architect, a good fifteen years older than myself. His name was Peter Grosscurth.

Unrealistic laws, or perhaps the lack of the same in Spain, were, as far as I could understand, both unclear and flexible at the time. A great deal of improvising was required to get the books to balance in this context, and it didn't help that additions and changes took place continuously, with or without retroactive effect.

Enough said, the above-mentioned Peter had on-going

challenges with the inhabitants who had already established themselves in the urbanization, as to which of the various common expenses they had to bear, as well as several practical details to do with the development itself. Practically speaking, this meant that a lot of them didn't pay anything at all.

As extenuating circumstances for those implicated, it must be mentioned that language and communication problems, as well as an understanding of the legislation, played a part.

One day, as Peter and I sat talking about the problem, which to me seemed totally crazy, I proposed that I make an objective attempt at mediating the conflict. After some decades as leader of a family business with up to 150 employees, I believed myself to possess a certain amount of experience in human relationships. The day came when I had gathered thirty or forty of the protesting clan for an information meeting. Food and drink had been organized and the atmosphere was good from the start. Peter was obviously not there, so it was just me and all the rest.

I had prepared myself well, I thought, and had committed everything to paper in order that nothing be left to chance.

Everyone listened without any form of interruption, and I felt that I had good control of the situation.

I believe my speech lasted about ten minutes whereupon I opened for a discussion about the arguments.

A few questions, for the sake of understanding, were raised here and there and answered, before I asked everyone to respect the laws, referring to everyone having to share the communal expenses to secure the future value of their respective investments.

After a short time where we continued the discussion in

groups, one of them came over to see me and said something like: "George, I speak on behalf of all of us. We largely agree with your argumentation and that you have put your case well, but you can tell Peter from all of us that we won't pay anything at all, before we are threatened by law to do so."

Neither before nor after have I heard such a collective opinion on something from so many different types of people.

What I didn't know at the time, however, but which later became clear to me, was that these people, who were mainly English, had previously been stationed in different countries around the world and had now settled here as pensioners. As the prices in Spain had already at this time made a great leap upwards, their economic situation had reached its breaking point.

In other words, it probably wasn't so much a lack of will as of possibility, and then, of course, it's important to maintain one's prestige.

It eventually ended up with many of the properties changing owners, and I don't really know what became of the hard core, but I hope at least that those who are still living after some twenty-five years, are doing well.

The regulations came into place eventually, the urbanization was fully legalized and these days it's neither misunderstood laws nor the government's responsibility that you are still doing battle – but so it is.

In the final analysis, people's divergent opinions, based on their different views on most things, is the reason for the on-going challenges in this little oasis. Fractions are formed and contrary views are put to the test.

For those of you who think this is an exception, take a closer look with this in mind, and see if it isn't also your opinion that this is reflected everywhere.

MY FOOD FOR THOUGHT ON
OPINIONS

OPINION

*You should decide early if you want to be remembered with a good
reputation or put all your energy into living.*
March 2019

OPINIONS I

*My Opinion is that it can be a good rule of thumb to keep your
Opinions to yourself and not be tempted to express them unless you
are sure they will not cause offence.*
July 2020

OPINIONS II

*It's good to have Opinions on most things - but only if you don't
claim they are the best.*
Sept. 2019

OPINIONS III

*Having opinions and being able to express them if you so wish is, at
least in the democracies I know of, a privilege worth fighting for.
It is a human right that must never be taken for granted.*
2014

RIGHT AND WRONG
August 1990

Or should the question rather be: Who is right and who is wrong? Yes, because that's really what most disputes are about. I simply claim that all of us are right based on our assumptions.

Is it thus as simple as saying that if everyone's assumptions were the same, you would no longer have any dispute about who is right or who is wrong? In other words, everyone would agree - thus no dispute.

Sounds simple, but so very far from reality.

Assumptions can be about possessing information. Then it naturally must be about interpreting the same information as well.

In this context it's natural to involve personal abilities and skills, as well as cultural and political backgrounds.

It's already clear to everyone that we're banging our heads against a brick wall - we just must admit that "all of us are right based on our assumptions".

Some – perhaps most of us –, think that we see something more clearly than others and thus believe: I know what's right and the others are wrong.

It is, of course, nice to be able to think about when going into the depth of things – or isn't it?

I believe most of us agree on this.

And now that we've reached the stage of awareness, what do we do?

Do we leave things as they are in our self-aggrandizement? That is, of course, the easiest, after all, we know deep down that we are right, don't we? And what it means is that the others are wrong, or does it?

If we are distant from the problems, we sneer a bit and add: Have you ever heard such nonsense; or, they can't possibly have a clue about what they're doing.

Such thoughts become easier the further away from the problems you are.

If the problems are of a more familiar character, it hurts in a different way and we are more careful of making our, at times, casual remarks.

Should we now ask ourselves the question: can I do something to influence, can I do something to soften the extremes?

A good expression is that "the truth normally lies somewhere in the middle".

What sort of skills are necessary to find the truth?

No, now he's getting completely off course. The truth doesn't exist, at least not if it diverges from my view.

Oops - here it comes again.

Can the word "objectivity" be used?

Let's chew on it a bit - objectivity - objectivity.

Doesn't it mean: seen with unbiased eyes; without taking sides; impartial; seen from the outside; bridging the gap?

Not bad, is it?

Imagine being able to withdraw, stand apart, and from that position calmly look at the problem.

Imagine being able to look at both sides; being self-critical as regards the information and thus the assumptions you hold about the case.

Imagine being large enough to let the one who seems to "swim the hardest" get the benefit of the doubt, before stating your conclusions.

Yes, imagine!

Isn't this what is, in other words, called mediation?

Is that why they're called diplomats, those strange people we normally only see in a black Mercedes with blue plates?

Are they called diplomats because they're trying to bridge the gap between countries, cultures, and religions?

Of course, that's why; we know it.

Yes, but then most of us know that they mainly talk incomprehensible gibberish, don't we?

Or is it like that?

No, let's just try to act a bit more objectively in our day-to-day lives, be a bit more diplomatic perhaps, just in a few situations each week.

Each one of us needn't stretch further before seeing that the world would be a far better place to live in.

P.S. Notice that in this Reflection, which I wrote in 1990, i.e. almost 35 years ago, I have mentioned the word "problem" four times. I have long since replaced the word "problem" with "challenge", which is what the first four Food for Thought on the next page are about. The next four are related to this Reflection: Right and wrong.

***

MY FOOD FOR THOUGHT ON
RIGHT AND WRONG

PROBLEM - CHALLENGE
A Problem can be complicated to solve. See the Problem as a challenge, and the solution becomes easier.
Sept. 2019

CHALLENGE IV
It's not just you who face Challenges, everyone does. It's the way you deal with them that's different.
Oct. 2019

PROBLEMS - CHALLENGES II
Everyone can recognize Problems when they see them. The art is to turn Problems into Challenges and to solve them.

PROBLEMS - CHALLENGES III
If you replace Problems with Challenges, it sounds much more positive. When faced with Challenges, the imagination is triggered, while the encounter with Problems may seem uninspiring.
March 2019

ABOUT BEING RIGHT
*Why not swallow your pride, if that's how it feels when you admit
that others are Right, and simply learn from it?
Why is it so important for most of us to be Right?
It's as if we constantly must convince ourselves that it is beneficial to
be Right while it is a defeat to be wrong.*

RIGHT AND WRONG I
*My simple claim is that everyone is right based on their assump-
tions. Is it as simple as saying that if only everyone had the same
assumptions, then we would no longer have the dispute about who
is right and who is wrong?*
August 1990

RIGHT AND WRONG II
*Being right based on one's assumptions is about possessing informa-
tion, and then of course it must also be about interpreting the same
information.*
August 1990

RIGHT AND WRONG III
*I know what is right and wrong and it is the others who are wrong,
many claim, and they feel good about that attitude. For them it
is of course the easiest. They believe deep down that they are right,
and that naturally means that the others are wrong. What they
have forgotten, however, are the assumptions, namely that they are
only right from their point of view.*
August 199

THE SMILE
May 1994

The smile gives you a feeling of warmth. It's always a relief when the smile appears, whether it's you yourself who are smiling or someone else.

Some people seem to be smiling permanently. It's not that kind of smile I'm thinking of, however; that kind seems to belong to an entire race of people, like in the Orient for instance.

No, I'm thinking of the smile we see daily on people we socialize with. That smile which you yourself, perhaps to a far greater extent than you do, should bring out.

The smile is warming, gives you a feeling of security. It's difficult to make contact with people who don't smile.

They don't necessarily suppress their smile on purpose, they probably are like that, don't understand the importance of the smile, in which case I feel sorry for them.

"Smile courses". Once again, we're talking about the smile which isn't so natural.

Millions and millions are spent by companies and organizations to promote themselves in a more positive way.

This is probably positive and perhaps even motivating for the employees. That's also not the kind of smile I'm thinking of, however.

The smile is something so personal, that if you have the slightest feeling it might not be real, it has a negative impact; you must be certain that the smile is real.

Be it from the slightly condescending smile we're all familiar with, to the one which stretches from ear to ear - the range is incredibly wide.

I've never thought about what the smile would be like without the eyes, but this reflection is not really about the eyes, it's about the smile.

Are we so used to the interaction between the eyes and the smile that it would be difficult to read expressions without that interaction, that is, with the smile alone?

I'll have to keep thinking about that.

Perhaps it's unfair to focus on the smile just on its own? Can the smile stand alone, be enough by itself?

Smile and the world smiles back at you, it is said.

There must be a lot of people who don't want the world smiling back at them.

***

MY FOOD FOR THOUGHT ON
THE SMILE

THE SMILE
A Smile is like sand on ice, it helps you walk more safely.

THE SMILE AND INSECURITY
The Smile is personal. If you feel Insecurity about its authenticity, it's negative. You must be sure that the Smile is genuine.

THE SMILE II
"Smile and the world smiles back at you", is a saying. There must be quite a few who do not want the world to smile on them.
May 1994

THE SMILE III
The smile warms, in a way gives a feeling of security. It's hard to connect with people who don't smile. It is not at all certain that they suppress the smile on purpose, they may just be like that, they don't understand the meaning of the smile. In that case, I pity them.
May 1994

THOUGHTS

October 1995

Are they just there or do we do something to make them appear?

My experience is that it's difficult to keep them in order, and that has probably something to do with concentration.

My thoughts race past in a constant flickering motion. When I put it like that, it's because I feel that there is a marked interaction between my thoughts and the visual image on my retina. I've never asked anyone else if they feel the same way.

It's a wonder that your thoughts don't boil over at times, but where would they go if they did?

You do, however, feel at times as though your thoughts are like steam in a pressure cooker, don't you? Especially when they are thoughts you have brooded over for a long time. They want out in one form or other and out they normally get.

Can, for instance, a burst of anger be the actual safety valve for a collection of aggressive thoughts?

If you are totally relaxed and just let your thoughts flow, which thoughts get priority, and which ingenious system docs the prioritizing?

Is this where the subconscious comes into it? Is it just another storehouse for thoughts?

Is it so that if you don't consciously suppress certain thoughts, you will be left with an even distribution of the different types?

It is undoubtedly a lot more pleasant to conjure up good thoughts, than to struggle with a predominance of bad ones. The latter can easily become a great strain if it happens over time.

The question is if it can be so easily controlled.

Here I believe it's important that you in yourself are reasonably balanced and that you have a platform to stand on, which isn't too slippery, and which gives your feet a good grip.

Thoughts are tax-free, it is said. It's important to take note of that.

It's a privilege we all have as human beings, that we can keep our thoughts to ourselves.

No one will ever get to know what you are thinking about if you want to keep it to yourself.

To share your thoughts with others can be good.

How often do we say: "Think of the time". Here you refer to thoughts about something or other, which you assume the person you are addressing has shared or heard about.

When you experience someone reading your thoughts, or when you feel that you yourself can read someone else's thoughts, it's probably more random or a result of being closely connected to the person and, thus, able to read his or her body language.

In connection with thoughts, I come to think about how good I feel right now.

Lying here relaxing after a hot bath and giving my thoughts free rein.

***

MY FOOD FOR THOUGHT ON THOUGHTS

THOUGHTS I

It is more pleasant to conjure up good Thoughts than to struggle with bad ones. The latter can become a strain if it becomes the norm.

1995

THOUGHTS II

When you struggle with Thoughts, they are normally both good and bad. Let your Thoughts flow freely when that happens; blockages can cause flooding.

May 2019

THOUGHTS III

It's said that "Thoughts are tax-free". Luckily so, otherwise I would be a poor man.

April 2019

THOUGHTS AND STEAM

Thoughts can be like Steam in a pressure cooker. They shall come out in some form or other.

Oct. 1995

TIME

April 1994

I'll do that when I retire, many people say; I'll have more time when I become a pensioner.

Nonsense. Do it now, I say.

That, of course, is impossible. It's only when you become a pensioner that you can do what you want to do now.

The decision seldom or never has to do with economy - always with time.

Time, the fourth dimension, perhaps humanity's most important concept.

Do we make the most of our time or, more accurately put, how do we make the most of our time?

We measure most things in what we get done and what we don't get done.

In any case, we blame it on time when we're dissatisfied, it's always time which is to blame, as if it's responsible for our inability to organize ourselves better.

Regardless of priority, there's always something which remains undone, something we would have liked to have done - time again.

We say we don't have time for this or that. The question of priority has a different meaning for each of us.

Poor old time, does it ever have a bad conscience?

My view of time is that I see it in relation to eternity, only ideally speaking, of course. I am probably quite realistic as regards to my own physical life here on earth, but I still like to see time from a "perspective of eternity".

Is it something to do with the fact that things live on? In that case, in which way and through what or whom, is not really of great significance. The most important for me is the belief that things live on.

History proves that things live on. I don't mean things I guess, they disappear, but time? History doesn't exist without time.

If something lasts forever it must be time and nothing but time.

Everything is regulated according to time. Absolutely everything. I can't think of a single thing which, in one form or other, isn't related to time.

Our time of birth is for astrologers crucial and determinate both for the way we are and for the way we develop. Here it hasn't got to do with just the day, the hour and the minute are also of the utmost significance.

Time is of the essence.

It was in the past that you had plenty of time. Was it perhaps less important to be on time for everything in those days, or did you have more time as, for instance, timetables weren't as developed as they are today?

Do opportunities create the rush for time?

With all the alternatives to be found for everything, it seems to be in the nature of things to have so much to be on time for.

Or is it the rush for time which creates the opportunities? What came first, the rush for time or the opportunities? Probably a balanced development.

Do we control time, or does it control us?

We compete in milliseconds - without time, no winners, and if there are no winners there are also no losers.

Does that mean that we can blame time for having losers? Someone must take the blame; everything becomes much easier then.

"Timing", it is said, is an important factor in all things. It means that the time aspect must be correct.

Despite all the analysis in the world, correct "timing" is difficult, if not impossible to calculate.

History repeats itself; it is said - rightly or wrongly. I don't know, but in my opinion, there is never a repetition, precisely because of time.

When the repetition takes place at a different time, it can't be the same which is being repeated. That makes me happy.

It's also good that we don't know too much about the future.

Time must be the greatest invention in the world.

***

**MY FOOD FOR THOUGHT ON
TIME**

TIME I

*It's not so important what Time it is - what's important is that it
passes.*

TIME II

*If there is something that lasts forever it must be Time and nothing
but the time.*
2018

TIME MUST TAKE THE BLAME

*We measure most things in what we get done and what we don't get
done. In any case, we Blame it on Time when we are dissatisfied.
It's always Time which is to Blame - as if it's responsible for our inability to organize ourselves better.*
2015

TIME III

*We compete in milliseconds - without Time,
no winners and no losers.*
April 1994

UNDERSTANDING II

2017

The wish of understanding and will to understand is fundamental. If you wish not to understand or reject the thought of understanding, no understanding is achieved, and so you can't expect to be understood either. You must have the wish and will to understand, to achieve understanding. In other words, understanding requires both wish and will.

Do you come further with understanding? After my opinion undoubtedly yes.

All decisions, if they should have any validity, must be based on understanding, and the wish and will to understand the content of the matter and the parties involved.

In many cases, it is much easier to keep the understanding in the background, not to use will, force and time to understand. Then, however the probability is great for the decisions to be of poor quality.

Imagine if it were only that simple and understandable.

Pundits are normally easy to understand. They often express simple, understandable postulates about this and that, but thanks to their personality they are normally categorised as unsympathetic.

Those, who on the other side acts consciously and keep the more modest style will normally be both respected and appreciated.

"Do you understand"? An expression often used when you expect a confirmation that the message is understood.

In my opinion, it can be too much on the commanding side. You take it for granted that the message is understood. A "yes" is expected as a confirmation.

For many it becomes difficult to say no, even if that is what they mean. For the one party this is of course correct, but what about the quality of the understanding.

Why not try with a little more weakened question? "I hope you have understood". This gives full admission to grasp eventual insecurity and may result in the following answer: "Yes, but I have a few questions". The dialogue is on, understanding substantiated, the communication is balanced, and basis laid for a compromised result.

Nit-picking many will say, especially in these times of SMS and e-mail where the most advanced communicators use a minimum of words with associated probability of misunderstandings. These days it has even gone so as that some TV channels squeeze information or messages into one line. To achieve this all kind of abbreviations are used, making it meaningless for us ordinary people. What happened to understanding? Well, the ones that understand it.

Most probably, only those of us of a "vintage age" are the ones who sigh. Every now and then, in debates, you will recognise someone assessing the following entry as an answer to a statement.

"I have a great deal of understanding for what you are saying, but…"

Well, I suppose it won't last long before this expression also disappears. It's much easier to say it directly: "I disagree with what you are saying".

I hope for some understanding of my view on the importance of understanding.

***

**MY FOOD FOR THOUGHT ON
UNDERSTANDING II**

UNDERSTANDING IV
*You can only do something with what you understand, but don't
forget that what you understand is seen from your point of view.*
April 2021

UNDERSTANDING V
*Understanding is one of the most important words we have. What
do you do with it?*
June 2021

UNDERSTANDING VI
*It is when you don't understand that you don't understand that the
real challenges start.*
July 2021

UNDERSTANDING VII
*The fact that you think others do not understand does not mean
that you are right in your own conviction that you are right.*
September 2020

ATTITUDES

2016

Without attitudes, I disregard the physical, and much would look different in our world.

It's probably not as if everybody has attitudes of the kind I'm thinking about, or more specifically said, conscious attitudes.

That is surely as it should be, but then it is also important that those with conscious attitudes stand up for them, and that may be more of a challenge.

"My attitude to that matter is". Dominant attitude: here it is about people with clear attitudes, at least in their own opinion, and they wish to express them.

Many certainly have attitudes that they seek to live up to in every way.

Those I think of do not always have to express their attitudes, they only have them, live up to them, and in view of that, they appear in the eyes of others as people with attitudes.

If you think about it, there are no limits to what attitudes you represent and observe with others.

Here I refer to seventeen Food For Thought which I hope can give you a more detailed understanding of my views on Attitudes:

***

MY FOOD FOR THOUGHT ON
ATTITUDES

BLACK – WHITE ATTITUDE
You simplify your views to an either/or.

HOPELESS AND HOPEFUL
As Hopeless, you can see no way other than giving up-
while as Hopeful you strive to reach the goal.

IMPERVIOUS AND INFLUENCE-ABLE
As Impervious, you steer straight forward without paying attention
to anything - while as Influenced you consider other's ideas and
thoughts.

TOLERANT AND INTOLERANT
As a Tolerant person you remain indulgent for the sake of domestic
peace - while as an Intolerant person you stand for your opinions to
highlight yourself.

2016

LOVING AND UNLOVING
As Loving, you turn the other cheek with a smile -
while as Unloving you do everything to reject further dialogue.

EVIL AND GOOD
As Evil, you want to see another's pain and suffering -
while as Good you do everything to make others feel better.

COMPASSIONATE AND INSENSITIVE

As a Compassionate person, you take an interest in another's situation with sympathy - while as Insensitive you have no interest in it.

CARESSING AND REPELLENT

As Caressing, you feel comfortable and want close contact - while as Repellent you clearly indicate the desire for physical distance.

ANGRY AND SOUR

As Angry you react with strong expressions - while as Sour, you are sad and not very talkative.

2016

FRIENDLY AND UNFRIENDLY

As Friendly, you slip easily into most environments - while as Unfriendly, you will be standing outside.

DOMINANT AND FLEXIBLE

As a Dominant, you stick to your point of view - while as Flexible you adapt to others.

MOODY AND HUMOROUS

As Moody you appear weak in a social context - while as Humorous you will be remembered as positive.

2016

NEGATIVE PERSONAL ATTITUDE

I feel pity for those who must step on others to keep themselves afloat.

March 2019

STRONG AND WEAK I

As Strong, you emphasize your Strengths - while if Weak you suppress them.

STRONG AND WEAK II

The Weakness of the Strong - may be the Strength of the Weak.

April 2019

ATTITUDE CHANGE

As long as the one-sided phrase: "What can I make of it?" is given first priority, no valuable progress is made.
"What can I contribute?", in a sensible balance with "What can I make of it?", is a better way forward.

February 2019

ATTITUDES

The most important thing is that you maintain your Attitudes if you are happy with them.

2019

***